Out of the Shadows

Studies in Modern European History

Frank J. Coppa
General Editor

Vol. 14

PETER LANG
New York • Washington, D.C./Baltimore
Bern • Frankfurt am Main • Berlin • Vienna • Paris

Shirley Elson Roessler

Out of the Shadows

Women and Politics
in the French Revolution, 1789–95

PETER LANG
New York • Washington, D.C./Baltimore
Bern • Frankfurt am Main • Berlin • Vienna • Paris

Library of Congress Cataloging-in-Publication Data

Elson Roessler, Shirley.
Out of the shadows: women and politics in the French
Revolution, 1789–95/ Shirley Elson Roessler.
p. cm. — (Studies in modern European history; vol. 14)
Includes bibliographical references.
1. France—History—Revolution, 1789–1799—Women.
2. Women in politics—France—History—18th century. 3. Women
revolutionaries—France—History—18th century. 4. Women's rights—
France—History—18th century. I. Title. II. Series.
DC158.8.E57   944.04'082—dc20   94-40970
ISBN 0-8204-2565-6 hardcover
ISBN 0-8204-4012-4 paperback
ISSN 0893-6897

Die Deutsche Bibliothek-CIP-Einheitsaufnahme

Elson Roessler, Shirley:
Out of the shadows: women and politics in the French
Revolution, 1789–95/ Shirley Elson Roessler.–New York; Washington,
D.C./Baltimore; Bern; Frankfurt am Main; Berlin; Vienna; Paris: Lang.
(Studies in modern European history; vol. 14)
ISBN 0-8204-2565-6 hardcover
ISBN 0-8204-4012-4 paperback
NE: GT

Cover design by James F. Brisson.

The paper in this book meets the guidelines for permanence and durability
of the Committee on Production Guidelines for Book Longevity
of the Council of Library Resources.

© 1998, 1996 Peter Lang Publishing, Inc., New York

Printed in the United States of America.

To Jill and Bernie
and in memory of my grandmothers,
Edith McKitrick Elson
and
Millicent Carbin Madden,
both pioneer women of Western Canada.

ACKNOWLEDGEMENTS

This book represents the combined efforts of many people. Although the authorship is mine, there have been others behind the scenes who have lent their loyal support in ways that made this endeavour possible. I am grateful to my family whose faith in my ability to finish this project never faltered; my husband, Karl, my children, Jill and Bernie, my mother, Kathleen Elson. I am grateful as well for the efforts of my friend and housekeeper, Froney Pearl Earle. I wish to thank Norman Jung for sharing his formidable typesetting skills and for many desperate computer rescue operations. Other friends and family within the university community who have been very supportive and helpful include Helen Buck, Xianguang Dai, Lydia Dugbazah, Joan Elson, Kathy Elson, Joseph Kozak, Kathleen MacDermott, Allen Pearson, Ulrich Trumpener, and Sinh Vinh. Their kindness and their generosity are greatly appreciated. As well, I wish to thank Frederick de Luna, Professor Emeritus, University of Alberta, who supervised the original version of this work.

TABLE OF CONTENTS

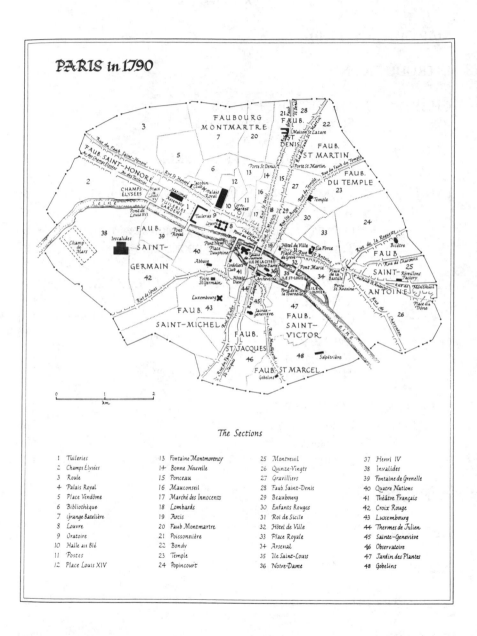

PARIS in 1790

The Sections

INTRODUCTION

T he topic of women's participation in the French Revolution has generally received little attention from historians, who have displayed a tendency to minimize the role of women in the major events of those years, or else to ignore it altogether. In the nineteenth century those who did attempt to deal with the topic chose to approach it with an emphasis on individual women who had for some reason attained a degree of notoriety. This *femmes célèbres* approach taken by such historians as Jules Michelet and E. Lairtullier succeeded mainly in removing the revolutionary women from the mainstream of history and isolating them in a manner that rendered them secondary in importance to male participants, who were considered to be the key characters in the *grandes journées* of the Revolution. Their work was valuable, however, in that it provided, in the case of Michelet, a general overview of the female role as well as details of the lives of some individual women. Lairtullier produced a comprehensive work that is still useful due to the wealth of detail that it contains.[1]

Other valuable studies of the female participants were written around the turn of the century. Léopold Lacour, Marc de Villiers, and Adrien Lasserre produced books which brought together some primary material in works of general interest.[2] Jeanne Bouvier, in 1931, continued in this tradition with a synthesis of primary material and interpretation which is still of interest.[3]

But the work of these historians, although valuable, has been largely neglected in general histories of the Revolution. Major researchers of a generation ago, which include Albert Soboul and Kare Tønnessen writing in French and George Rudé in English, also concentrated on the male *sans-culottes* (working class men) to the almost total neglect of the group which formed their counterpart, the female *sans-culotterie.*[4]

In recent decades historians have produced some worthwhile general studies of the women's role in the Revolution, but most of these are only of article length.[5] In 1979 Darlene Levy, Harriet Applewhite, and Mary Durham Johnson produced a collection of documents which, although valuable in itself, left much room for analysis and development.[6] In French, Paule Marie Duhet published a book in 1971 on the women of the Revolution that contains some valuable material but is extremely sketchy on the events of the October Days of 1789 and omits entirely the important events of 1795.[7] Another recent French book that has no counterpart in English is Maria Cerati's monograph on the activities of the *Société des Citoyennes Républicaines Révolutionaires.*[8] There also have been good biographies published in recent years which deal with lives of the more famous women of the period.[9]

Recently, in anticipation of or concomitant with the celebration of the Bicentenary, some general books on the women of the Revolution have appeared. In French, these include works by Anne Soprani, Nicole Vray, Catherine Marand-Fouquet, and Annette Rosa.[10] In English, Linda Kelly produced a book of general interest which contains biographical information on several of the *femmes célèbres.*[11] Written for popular audiences, however, these works are based on little original research in primary sources and are not extensively documented. One major scholarly contribution among these books, however, is that of the French historian Dominique Godineau, who in 1988 produced a thorough study at last of the female *sans-culottes* of Paris, whom she called the *citoyennes tricoteuses*.[12] Godineau's work reflects prodigious, accurate research and careful, intelligent analyses and interpretations of primary material. An article by Godineau on the same topic is now available in English, along with another general article on women in the Revolution by Levy and Applewhite.[13] Olwen Hufton, in 1992, produced a brief work on the topic which deals in part with the political role of women in the Revolution.[14] During the same year, Sara Melzer and Leslie Rabine published a collection of articles dealing with the topic of women.[15]

Despite these various works on women in the Revolution, one cannot help but notice that the topic is still largely ignored in recent general histories. J. F. Bosher, for example, considers women only infrequently and in a very general manner, and like his predecessors, has failed to incorporate valuable information from recent works. The general studies of the French Revolution by William Doyle and Owen Connelly also treat female participation only cursorily.[16] Simon Schama has dealt in considerable detail with some of the activities of the women, but his work is semi-popular in appeal, and is not free of errors; moreover, Schama's book ends with Thermidor and thus omits one of the most important periods of female activity during 1795.[17] Even the major contribution by French historians to the Bicentenary publications, the *Dictionnaire critique de la Révolution française* edited by Francois Furet and Mona Ozouf, contains very little about women. The only articles on women therein are devoted to Queen Marie Antoinette and Madame de Staël, and the long article on the *Clubs and sociétés populaires* completely ignores the women's organizations.[18]

Some of the recent works on the topic focus on feminist issues and seem to dwell on the idea that these women were motivated above all by economic concerns. The contribution of Olwen Hufton and Ruth Graham are not entirely free of the old idea of women as a group of termagants *(furies)* and/or shrews *(mégères)* preoccupied with the search for food. The image of Madame Defarge dies hard as does the belief that food is an issue of strictly female concern.

Thus despite the various kinds of research and publication on the topic, there is still a need for a more general and scholarly study of the role of women during the French Revolution. This book attempts to meet this need by focusing on the political participation of women in the main revolutionary arena. It is by no means a complete history of the Revolution, nor even a complete history of the role of women in it. Rather, it examines major topics involving women as political participants and attempts to illustrate the importance of their activities in determining the directions taken by the Revolution in the years between 1789 and 1795.

The first of these major topics is the October Days, which is the only well-known example of female activity during the Revolution. But while this topic is familiar, my research has shown that even in this event the role of women has not been adequately examined. Certainly the work of George Rudé, which offers one of the most detailed analysis of the role of women, leaves much that is unexplored. Chapter 1 offers an extended analysis of the events of October, 1789 and brings out many significant details lacking in most accounts.

In subsequent chapters the participation of women in that most characterisic aspect of the Revolution, the club movement, is explored. Chapter 2 examines the women's political activity between October, 1789 and the spring of 1793 when the most influential of the strictly female political clubs, the *Société des Citoyennes Républicaines Révolutionnaires,* was organized in Paris. The next chapter is devoted to an analysis of the history of that significant organization. Chapter 4 looks in detail at the final phase of female collective action in the Revolution, the days of Germinal and Prairial in the Year III (spring 1795). My research shows that these events were far more important than the brief return of women to the revolutionary stage as has been suggested.[19]

As sources I have consulted some archival material, but the most valuable of my primary sources proved to be some that have long been available to scholars but that have never before been fully exploited for the study of women's political involvement in the Revolution. These include above all the files of *Le Moniteur universel,* which contain not only the proceedings of the various revolutionary assemblies but also much other valuable information about the women's attitudes, behaviour, and burgeoning political awareness throughout the years of revolutionary activity. For some of the parliamentary debates the scholarly edition, *Les Archives parlementaires,* also proved to be of great value.

Besides the *Moniteur*, there are other contemporary periodicals which contain much information relevant to women. Those I have consulted include *Les Révolutions de Paris, Révolutions de France et de Brabant, L'Ami du Peuple, Le Babillard, Le Courrier de l'Hymen, La Gazette des Halles, La Feuille du Soir, Les Etrennes*

Nationales des Dames, La Bouche de Fer, La Mère Duchesne, and *Journal de Lyon.* Other primary sources which I have used for information on the women's activities include the proceedings of the Paris Jacobin Club, as compiled by Alphonse Aulard, and the collection of documents that he edited for the period following Thermidor.[20] Alexandre Tuetey's massive collection of archival documents on Paris during the Revolution has also been very valuable.[21] Among other valuable primary sources is the report of the official inquiry in 1790 into events of and participants in the October Days, which is a repository of information that a number of historians have cited but which appears to have been directly consulted but rarely.[22]

In combination with a variety of other primary material available in printed form, these sources have made it possible to piece together a picture of the women's contribution in some totality and with a wealth of detail. This research suggests that women played a role of far greater magnitude in the political arena of the Revolution than that which has so far been attributed to them.

CHAPTER ONE

THE OCTOBER DAYS

Les hommes ont fait le 14 juillet, les femmes le 6 octobre. Les hommes ont pris la Bastille royale, et les femmes ont pris la royauté elle-même. (The men made the 14 July; the women the 6 October. The men took the royal Bastille and the women took royalty itself.) Jules Michelet, *Les Femmes de la révolution.*

FROM PARIS TO VERSAILLES

Women played no role in the fiscal and political crises that led to the convocation of the Estates-General in 1789. However, they soon began to participate in some of the most significant events of that first year of the Revolution. Working women had sensed for some time that their traditional rights and roles were gradually being eroded by state intervention. Their traditional rights within the guilds and their participation in religious and secular ceremonies were, they felt, increasingly the object of such intervention. The feeling of loss of control in their daily lives resulted in the formulation of petitions by groups of women in which they expressed grievances; the famous *Cahiers des doléances* (Notebooks of grievances) taken early in 1789 testified to the growing discontent of the working class women of Paris. The flower-sellers, the laundresses, even the unhappily married women, had their say in the *Cahiers*.[1] At the same time, women were experiencing increasing difficulty in obtaining enough food to feed their families. Wages were low and bread was scarce and in April a few women registered their discontent with the situation by participating in the Réveillon Riots in Paris. Even at this early stage a political theme surfaced along with the economic issues. A woman, Marie-Jeanne Trumeau, was charged with inciting the rioters by cheering the third estate. She was sentenced to death but was subsequently reprieved because she was pregnant[2]

The attack on the Bastille on 14 July, 1789 was predominantly a male affair. However, there can be little doubt that there were women present. Marie Charpentier Hauserne, a laundress, was afterwards officially honored as one of the nine hundred *vainqueurs de la Bastille* (conquerors of the Bastille). Pauline Léon, later to be president of the *Société des Citoyennes Républicaines Révolutionnaires,* was in the streets that day, erecting barricades. Contemporary prints show several women, armed, among the insurgents, who had the support not only of the entire population of the Faubourg Saint-Antoine, but of Paris as a whole.[3]

Throughout the first summer of the Revolution groups of women formed huge processions of a religious nature in which market women and laundresses wound their way through the streets of Paris to the doors of the church of *Sainte Geneviève.* These processions, although orderly and disciplined in appearance, were regarded by clergy and nobility as menacing in that they seemed to indicate, or even fore-shadow, an intention of a participation of a more violent kind.[4]

On 4 October, 1789, against this backdrop of increasing unrest, word of an event which had taken place at Versailles three days ear-lier reached Paris. What had begun as a gathering of troops had escalated into a raucous celebration. In the course of the evening the tricolor cockade, symbol of the new French nation, had been insulted with the apparent approbation of the queen. Due to conditions exist-ing in Paris, the food shortages and general uncertainty about the political situation, the incident at Versailles served to fuel an already smouldering conflict, and remarkably enough, the most intense reaction came from the female population of Paris. The response came in the form of a determined group action which displayed strong political overtones from the outset and which marked the beginning of a burgeoning political awareness among the women. Maturation of women's political responsibility would blossom during the years of revolutionary struggle which were to follow and which would eventually reach its height in the spring days of 1795. However, events were to show that the seeds of a female political understanding were already present during the October Days of 1789.

Those days, historians agree, were essentially women's days. Exactly why the women responded with such energy and determination at this particular time has been the subject of debate as has been the reasons for the sudden intersection of political and economic interest which occurred during these days. The women realized, it seems, albeit in a somewhat simplistic way, that political intervention was the means to practical reform, a reform that was becoming more crucial momentarily as the threat of famine worsened in the capital.[5] Although the harvest of 1789 had been good, at least in the Paris region, grain was in short supply for several reasons; the milling process had been delayed by lack of wind and a partial drought, fear of state bankruptcy encouraged hoarding of money, and bread prices remained high.[6] There were so many problems related to the circulation of grain that contemporary journals complained that they were unable to report on the situation in detail.[7] Reports of widespread hoarding circulated in the capital and by late summer the feeling in Paris was one of near panic. Violent incidents were increasing daily as the population struggled to obtain food and to force a fair and equitable distribution of the same.

Women were noticeably present in the crowds which acted out their frustration in the weeks preceding the October crisis. During the night of 1-2 August the deputy mayor of Saint-Denis, Chatel, was stabbed to death in a popular riot caused by people demanding a reduction in the price of bread. Chatel had refused their request and had made derogatory remarks about the crowd, calling them *canaille* (rabble). Among those arrested was at least one woman.[8] Incidents involving seizure of grain carts attempting to provision the city also increased during this period. On September 16 women stopped five carts of grain at Chaillot and brought them to the Hôtel de Ville. There the women complained that the men understood nothing and stated that they wished to participate in the events. The women repeated the performance the next day at the Place des Trois Maries.[9] The *Moniteur* reported that as the scarcity of food increased so did the number of deaths directly attributable to starvation. During the night of 22-23 September there were fewer than thirty sacks of grain at the Halle de la Ville in Paris. Although four or five hundred sacks arrived in the early morning hours there still existed a shortage of flour and therefore of bread.

On a typical day in Paris, the crowds would begin to gather at the bakers' shops at four a.m. Men, women, children, the elderly all began the day by "arming against famine." Bread bought, or rather "conquered," with ready money was a victory. Many wage earners lost their day's pay because they were still in the bread line in the late afternoon. Having been unable the day before to appease the hunger which devoured them, they would be back in the bread line the next morning without money or strength, "squeezed between need and

despair."[10] The inadequacy of the food supply, the clumsy and unfair system of distribution, the shortage of money, and the demise of
luxury industry with the resulting rise in unemployment, all contributed to the bleak prospects of Parisians.

In the face of this escalating hardship women were making a val-
iant effort to feed their families. But they were also struggling to
understand the political tension which held all Paris in its grip. In so
doing they reached far beyond the boundaries of their traditional
domain. The women knew that the king had continually resisted the
work of the Revolution, that he had refused to give up the royal veto,
to sign the Declaration of the Rights of Man and Citizen, and to sanc-
tion the decrees of the night of 4 August which would put an end to
feudalism in France. The women were not unmoved by the message
inherent in the king's actions and to further aggravate the situation
persistent rumours were circulating that an aristocratic plot involving the queen was forming at court with the objective of putting an
end to the Revolution. As well, the women could not help but notice
a marked increase in the number of soldiers in the area of Paris and
Versailles during the last days of September.

When the details of the "orgy" at Versailles reached Paris, the
women were already prepared to act. Their approach to king and
court had been a certainty for several days. Testimony given later at
an inquiry into the events of October (the Châtelet) showed that hunger was undeniably a factor in the women's action. Some of them
arrived at Versailles as living embodiments of the famine that af-
flicted Paris. Some complained to the king that they had been thirty-
six hours without food. They responded to the king's offer of money
by stating that it was not money but food that they needed.[11]   But

concern for matters other than food was certainly evident as well. In Paris it was known that the murmurings of women indicated that they believed that the source of evil was at Versailles and that it was necessary "to seek out the king and to bring him to Paris."[12] Some of the women expressed their animosity toward the queen as the perpetrator of traitorous plots and of their personal misery, wishing openly to have the opportunity to insult her, and a few even threatened to kill her. A female witness before the inquiry stated that one woman expressed the desire "to carry the queen's head on the end of a sword."[13]

How and where did the events begin that were to result in such testimony? They began in two separate districts of Paris on the morning of 5 October. The women of Les Halles, which housed the central markets, and the Faubourg St. Antoine, the district of the furniture builders of Paris, rose in revolt. The movement began when a young girl ran into a guardhouse and seized a drum. She marched around adjacent streets beating the drum and shouting about the scarcity of bread. The women began to respond, gathering first as a small group which soon increased in size. It headed in the direction of the Hôtel de Ville.[14] In the Faubourg St. Antoine, a persistent woman forced the sexton of the church of St. Marguerite to ring the church bells. The parish priest had refused to comply when two men made the same request a few minutes earlier. The woman succeeded where the men had failed.[15]

In response to the drum and the bells, more women began to congregate in groups and to make their way toward the Place de Grève. They began arriving at about nine a.m. On the way there one group accosted a luckless baker whose two-pound loaf had been found to be seven ounces short. He narrowly escaped with his life as many in the group wished to string him from the lamp post.[16]   Once at the Hôtel de Ville the women's intentions became obvious to bystanders. The members of the group wished to complain to officials of the commune about their negligence and ineptitude in provisioning the city. It was noted that the women's intentions soon shifted and their only interest was in obtaining permission to go to Versailles.[17]

The courtyard of the Hôtel de Ville was not well guarded on the morning of 5 October. Jean-Sylvain Bailly, mayor of Paris, had been on guard there throughout the night in anticipation of trouble. At about five a.m. he left for home after dismissing the members of the National Guard who were on duty there. By the time the women began arriving at about eight a.m. only two commissioners were on duty. The first group of women that entered the courtyard were reported to be young, dressed in white, well-groomed, with an "air of gaiety" about them. This group was quite well-behaved, curious but polite, with seemingly no "bad intentions."[18]   Their immediate interest was neither food nor politics but a simple curiosity about the building itself. They explored the various rooms of the Hôtel de Ville and asked about the purpose of each. They even asked for assistance for some members of the group who were finding the whole undertaking to be too much for them. Some of these had been forced to come, others were pregnant, and some simply were not feeling well. The women asked some of the men present to look after these people, to let them sit down and to help them if necessary. The women were said to have displayed an almost childlike curiosity and spirit as they entered and investigated the building.[19]

In other areas of the complex the crowd was not so peaceful. The unfortunate soul in charge of the arms store at the Hôtel de Ville complained that he had been the victim of a violent crowd of women who ransacked his area looking for weapons. The women helped themselves to a variety of firearms and then the crowd spread throughout the building. Later, this witness was dragged up to a clock tower and narrowly escaped being hanged or garrotted. A woman in the crowd rescued him by cutting the cord that had been tied around his neck.[20]

The women apparently began breaking down doors and gathering up papers. They were heard to complain that paperwork was all that had been accomplished during the epoque of the Revolution. They expressed the intention of burning all this paper and in all probability the whole building would have gone up with it.[21] The crowd was becoming increasingly more determined with the women in the forefront of the action, although by now some men were present inside the building. All weapons were turned over to the women and many more arrived with torches. Many of the women demanded bread and some proclaimed that the Commune (city council) was composed of bad people who should all be strung up. Bailly, the mayor, and Lafayette, commander of the National Guard, should be the first.[22] The women sang and danced in the courtyard while demanding to know their whereabouts. One of the crowd was heard to complain that members of the city council were all in league with the king.[23]

There can be little doubt that the women had intentions of a more comprehensive nature as well. An account of events given in a contemporary journal, *Evénement de Paris et Versailles*, illustrates that some women were at this point already thinking in both economic and political terms. Although their attitudes were not always consistent one with another and may not have shown any great sophistication as yet, they were rooted in an undeniable practicality and illustrated a growing desire for political intervention to change the existing situation. Some wished to know why bread was so difficult to obtain and why it was so costly. Others wanted the king and queen to come to Paris to live at the Louvre where "they would do infinitely better than at Versailles." Still others wanted all black cockades proscribed. These were symbols of the House of Habsburg, the family of the unpopular queen, Marie-Antoinette. Others asked that the Flanders regiment, which had been gathered ominously around the city since June, be sent away along with the bodyguards of the king. The king and queen, some thought, should have the Parisian National Guard for their defence.[24] The National Guard's commanding officers, meanwhile, found themselves in mortal danger at the hands of a hostile crowd which was infuriated by its inability to gather more arms and ammunition.[25]

As the morning wore on the women became increasingly determined to go to Versailles. They selected Stanislas-Marie Maillard who was one of the heroes of the Bastille to be their leader and they decided to go in groups to various areas of the city and recruit other women to march with them. They agreed to meet at Place Louis XV (later Place de la Concorde) and to proceed on their way from there.[26] Some of the women showed great enthusiasm for joining the march. The woman Cheret was one of these. In a later testimony she described her actions, reporting that she left her "virtuous mother" abruptly, abandoning her plans, and joined with the citizenesses who were going to Versailles under the leadership of Pierre-Augustin Hulin and Maillard and some other heroes of the Bastille.[27]

The women left the Hôtel de Ville at approximately eleven a.m., accompanied by resounding cries of "Bread and to Versailles!" Many of the women arriving now at the Place de Grève were armed with pikes, brooms, spears, and other such instruments. Cannons were loaded onto wagons and one witness testified that there were many women in the crowd, which left for Versailles resembling an army of crusaders.[28]   Bailly also witnessed the departure and reported that the women who left at eleven a.m. recruited, willingly or unwillingly, all the women that they met along the way. He described the entourage. "Cannons followed the crowd, supported on wagons which the women had obtained for this purpose. They carried as well gunpowder and bullets. Some were driving the horses, others were seated on the cannons and were holding the fuses in their hands." Bailly estimated the size of the crowd at about four thousand women and about four to five hundred men.[29]

The trip itself was an eventful one. Several incidents along the way illustrate that the women were struggling to make sense of the political realities of their situation. Their hostility to the monarchy erupted on several occasions although generally they attempted to show respect for that institution, despite their doubts and complaints. As well the women were ambivalent about the calibre of leadership that Maillard was providing and they challenged it several times during the march. The group made its way along the quai Orfèvres up to the gate of the Louvre and it was here that the women had their first major disagreement with Maillard. He did not wish to cross the Tuileries garden on the grounds that the Swiss guards would oppose such an action and that it would be an insult to the king to have such a large number of people invade the gardens.[30]   The women rejected

The Women Leave for Versailles, October 5, 1789. (Stamp) Courtesy Musée Carnavalet.

his suggestion that they remain outside the garden and suggested in their turn that he might like to resign as leader if he did not wish to conform to their wishes. At the same time it became evident, he said, that "some among them wished to hit him." This caused Maillard, prudently, to change his stance. He was obliged, he said, to tell them that he would bow to their wishes but that they must allow him to exercise all the prudence demanded by such an ill-considered action as crossing the gardens of the king. The women agreed.[31]

The trip across the Tuileries was not without its drama. An altercation did take place with one of the Swiss guards. Jeanne Martin Lavarenne was assigned by Maillard to go ahead of the group and warn the guard that the women were coming. She was to explain that there was nothing to fear and that the women would behave. Unfortunately, this tactic failed because the Swiss guard refused to listen and proceeded to draw his sword and pursue the messenger. Madame Lavarenne was armed only with a broom and she shouted for help. Maillard reported that the other women wished to kill the guard and it was thanks to his powers of persuasion that the guard was ultimately spared. Maillard liked to look capable and not unpatriotic. He pointed out to the women that the guard represented the person of the king and was himself worthy of respect. The guard soon proved that he was in no mood for debate. He directed blows at Maillard who was in turn rescued by Madame Lavarenne. She delivered such a blow with her broom to the crossed swords of the men that they were both disarmed. One of the other women stepped in and knocked the guard to the ground. Another one was armed with a musket equipped with a bayonet. This one had intentions of finishing off the guard when Maillard intervened to save him.[32] At this point it appears that the women's survival skills were more keenly honed than their political sensibilities. Later, Madame Lavarenne found it expedient to testify that she was forced to march with the women who had threatened to beat her if she didn't cooperate. According to her she had drawn on a whole arsenal of excuses to avoid the whole affair. She told the women that she had not eaten and she had no money and it simply would not be possible for her to accompany them. This account was a far cry from her enthusiastic participation in the Tuileries incident.[33]

The Place Louis XV proved to be inadequate for the rendezvous before the actual march and the women met instead at the Place d'Armes. The array of weapons was colourful. They carried everything from broomsticks and mops to rifles with spears, as well as forks, swords, and pistols. They had no ammunition but hoped to go the the Arsenal and find some there. Maillard dissuaded them from carrying through this project by explaining that since they only wished to ask for bread and justice at the National Assembly it was hardly appropriate to bear arms. He convinced them, or so he later claimed, that they would fare better at Versailles if they did not use force. Eventually most of them conceded and put down their arms and any who did not were forcibly disarmed by the others who announced that there would be no exceptions. Maillard was later to boast that by now the women had such confidence in him that they announced unanimously that they would tolerate no leader but him and all other men in the group must walk at the rear of the procession. About twenty women were said to have marshalled the men into line.[34]

The group left the Place d'Armes and took the route to Versailles with eight or ten drummers leading the procession. Six or seven thousand women appear to have been present although the exact number is difficult to estimate. The group passed through Chaillot, making its way along the Seine. Most of the houses were locked up in anticipation of the approaching mob. Despite the fact that everything was tightly closed the women began knocking on doors and were fully prepared to force their way in if necessary. They were reprimanded by Maillard who admonished them that this was not an honourable way to behave and he warned them that he would resign as their leader if they persisted in such activity. Maillard also took this opportunity to caution the women that such behaviour would cause them to be negatively regarded at Versailles. On the other hand, he said, if they were to proceed peacefully and honestly, they would be welcomed there.[35] The women were obviously determined in their actions to the point of becoming unruly. Constant reminders to stay within the limits of the law were required to keep them on track.

As the group approached Sèvres rumours reached it that the bridge was closed and that all the houses and businesses were locked up. No food or drink would be available for the women. This proved indeed to be the case and the women responded with outrage. They were prepared to break down doors and take what they wanted. The armed men who arrived on the scene were sympathetic to the women and it was reported that they did not protect the property of the citizens of Sèvres as they were supposed to, but rather assisted the women in finding refreshments. They helped Maillard obtain a small amount of bread and wine. The women settled down and some even were able to pay for the wine. In his testimony before the Châtelet, Maillard was to testify that his only regret was that he could not supply his companions with more sustenance.[36]

The group retook the road to Versailles and passed through Viroflay where they met several men on horseback who appeared to be bourgeois. They had black cockades pinned to their hats. These symbols of the House of Habsburg and support for the queen Marie Antoinette were sufficient to enrage the women. Some threatened to kill these men in retaliation for insulting the national cockade. One was knocked off his horse and the cockade wrenched from his hat.[37] He was rescued by Maillard who worked out a deal with the women. It was proposed that his life would be spared if he agreed to give up his horse and walk at the back of the procession wearing a sign which identified him as one who had insulted the national cockade. The unfortunate victim agreed to everything. One of the women immediately mounted his horse and rode off toward Versailles to announce the imminent arrival of the Parisians.[38]

Not long afterward the group entered the wide avenue leading into the city. There they encountered two more men dressed as bourgeois and wearing black cockades on round hats. Some of the women immediately took the hats and gave the cockades to Maillard. Two of the women mounted the horses with the men on behind them and proceeded down the avenue. After this the cannons were moved to the back of the procession and the women entered the city in a non-menacing way. They made their entrance shouting "Long live Henry IV!" and "Long live the king!" In return they were greeted with "Long live our *Parisiennes* !" from the crowds along the avenue.[39]

The crowd began to separate into smaller groups once it had entered the city. It was pouring rain by the time the crowd made its way down the avenue and some of the group later reported that they stopped in a cabaret. While sharing a bottle of wine a couple of them recognized a woman that they knew who lived in Versailles. She offered shelter for the night to eight of the women from Paris.[40] Others carried on to the Place d'Armes and met up with the king's body guards who blocked the way. One woman received a cut on the finger in the fracas that followed. The guards were apparently in battle formation and were ready to take on the mob, be it male or female, armed or unarmed.

Madame de la Tour du Pin, one of the queen's ladies-in-waiting, gave one of the best eye-witness accounts of the group's arrival from the royalist point of view. She described how protection against the oncoming mob was arranged at Versailles. The National Guard had been called to assemble at the Place d'Armes. They arranged them-selves for battle with their backs to the grill which surrounded the royal courtyard. All gates and entrances to the chateau were closed and "gates which had not turned on their hinges since the time of Louis XIV were locked for the first time." The king had returned with haste from hunting when apprised of the women's approach. He arrived at Versailles at about three o'clock. It was shortly there-after, at about five or six o'clock, that the first of the crowd of women entered the city. In the rain and gathering darkness they made their way up the avenue to the door of the National Assembly in the Salle des Menus Plaisirs. Many of them entered. Here they expressed their two-fold wishes to the assembled deputies. They wanted bread and they wished to take the deputies to Paris.[41]

In the National Assembly

A deputy from Paris, Guy Jean-Baptiste Target, had just finished speaking when the women entered. They presented themselves at the bar of the Assembly with Maillard at their head and he took the floor.[42] Jean-Joseph Mounier, deputy from Grenoble, was in the chair. He allowed the women to enter, about twenty of them, he was later to report, and he requested that "they not disturb the public tranquillity." He assured them that the king and the National Assembly would do all in their power to provision the city of Paris with the necessities of life.[43]

At first the women were quite tractable inside the Assembly. They knew the importance of their mission and were determined to behave and to be heard. Their entry interrupted a discussion of food shortages in Paris, so their timing was impeccable. Maillard instructed them to be quiet and Mounier permitted them to address the deputies through Maillard who first requested that the bodyguards of the king should redress the wrong that they had done to the national cockade on 1 October. This caused a general disturbance within the Assembly, with several deputies shouting that the guards had never insulted the cockade. They also shouted that the wish for citizenship could not be forced and had to be undertaken of one's own free will. It must stem from the desire to be one with the Nation. Displaying the three black cockades taken on the road to Versailles, Maillard stated that it was an honour to be a citizen and any member who did not feel honoured by that title should be excluded immediately from the Assembly. This expression of patriotism apparently drew great applause

from those present as shouts of agreement arose from all sides.[44]   The
women were deeply involved in these emotional displays.   When
Maillard was given a national cockade by some of the bodyguards,
the women cheered and shouted, "Long live the king and the bodyguards!" When Maillard began to address the problem of the large
number of troops in the vicinity of Paris and Versailles, the women
listened attentively. He described the uneasiness that this situation
had caused in Paris. He said that in order to prevent trouble and to
allay the fears of the people of Paris, the Flanders regiment should be
sent away "because the citizens fear a revolution from them." The
president assured the group that he would advise the king of its concerns and Maillard went on to emphasize that in this time of calamity
and of such shortages of bread the regiment would be better off in
one of the provincial cities rather than so close to the capital where
bread was so expensive.[45]

The next topic of discussion was that of the possibility of an audience with the king. This had been one of the goals of the women
from the outset. Mounier thought it would be best to delay any meeting because the king had just returned from the hunt. Maillard was
able to convince him otherwise, stating that the king was already
aware that the women of Paris were at Versailles "in great numbers"
and that would certainly cause him to worry. Mounier agreed but
admonished the women to be patient because this situation could not
be resolved in a hurry.[46] The decision to approach the king resulted
in a delegation composed of a dozen deputies and Mounier, who
consented to have some of the women accompany them.[47]

The scene in the National Assembly after the deputation left was
one of confusion. The remaining women broke the protocol of the

Parisian Women in the National Assembly. (Anonymous) Courtesy Musée Carnavalet.

meeting, initially with an expression of hostility to the clergy and later with a display of aggression toward the deputies themselves. An abbot wearing a cross tried to kiss the hand of one of the women, who responded with disrespect and rage, and who expressed her feelings in obscene terms and delivered a blow to the offending abbot. The group then shouted disrespectfully at the deputies, "Down with the priests. It is all the clergy who have made our misfortune." The political reason for the women's behaviour was explained by Maillard. Their hostility resulted from rumours in Paris that the clergy was blocking the Assembly's efforts to make a constitution. One of the deputies, who was seated to the left of the acting president, was obviously annoyed with the attitude of the women. He declared in no uncertain terms that when a stranger enters the Assembly and insults its members, immediate punishment is necessary. Maillard hastened to explain that his intentions were innocent and that he had no desire to malign any member of the Assembly. He felt that quite to the contrary he was giving the clergy an opportunity to defend itself and had only brought the matter up in order to prevent further disorder in the Assembly. At this time Maximilian Robespierre, deputy from Arras, made a patriotic speech which apparently calmed the women, at least for the moment.[48]

In the meantime the women waiting outside the Assembly had become extremely agitated because of a rumour that Maillard had been poisoned. Maillard had to hurry outside to reassure them that he was still with them. After receiving this assurance the women decided that they would all come inside the Assembly. Maillard told them that it would be neither possible nor necessary for them to do so because at this point they had been successful anyway and he assured them that the peaceful approach taken was much better than to have shed blood "as they had wished in the capital and on the way." At this the women promised that all would be tranquil from then on.[49]

However, the altercation which soon took place belied their promise. The women engaged in an argument with the bodyguards and shots were fired. The women asked Maillard's opinion on the type of death that one of the bodyguards warranted as they had him in custody and were planning to do away with him. The women were holding the bodyguard's horse by the bridle and were threatening him with serious injury. He managed to escape and Maillard cautioned the women about their behaviour and warned them not to go any closer to the chateau.[50]

THE WOMEN CAPTURE THEIR KING

The group of intruders inside the Assembly continued to grow and became increasingly disruptive in their actions. They spoke loudly to the persons in the galleries and some surrounded the president's chair. The chair was occupied by the Bishop of Langres in Mounier's absence and several of the women embraced the bishop and some of the deputies as well.[51] Later, the women, who now constituted a crowd in the room, interrupted the attempt made by the assembly to discuss a matter pertaining to the criminal code. They insisted upon returning to a discussion of food supply. They shouted, "And of what importance to us is criminal jurisprudence when Paris is without bread?" At this Mirabeau rose and requested that the president "retain the dignity" of the deliberations by ordering all the strangers in the hall to get out. He complained that "The representatives of the nation are not able to discuss wisely in the midst of scandalous tumult." When one deputy suggested that the Assembly should meet elsewhere, Mirabeau responded that it would not be appropriate, or even wise, for the deputies to desert their posts the moment dangers, imaginary or real, appeared to menace the public good.[52] These words appear to have made an impression on the women and they kept silent. The deputies were able to deliberate until four in the morning.[53]

Meanwhile, the small group of deputies and women were making their way to the chateau to present their case to the king. Mounier described the journey in some detail in his *Memoires.* He said that they were on foot, in the mud, with a strong rain. The sides of the avenue leading to the chateau were lined with people. The women with him were divided into several groups.[54] He reported that they were well-received at the chateau but instead of the six women to whom he had promised entry, he had to admit a dozen.[55] At least two of the women who were admitted to the chateau did not arrive there with the delegation from the National Assembly. One of these was Françoise Rolin who later was to testify before the Châtelet that she was with Louise Chabry, a flower-seller from Paris, and that they had remained in the Place d'Armes after entering Versailles. She stated that from there they saw a group of about five men dressed in black making their way toward the chateau. They were followed, she said, by many of the women that had come from Paris in the same crowd as she had. She and Chabry approached the men and obtained permission to accompany them and she was to be one of four women admitted to see the king.[56] Louise Chabry's account of the incident is somewhat different. She said that five, not four, women were admitted along with the deputies and that she was the one who presented the complaints "of the women and of the people" to the king, for the purpose of demanding of him "bread and the necessities of life." She testified as well that the king had received them in a most friendly manner but she gave no details of the discussion which took place. She did say, however, that she grew weak in the presence of the king and that he gave her wine in a golden goblet.[57] Mounier's testimony reveals that the only topic of discussion was the problem of the shortage of staples in Paris. [58]

Rolin testified that while Chabry went in with the others to meet the king, she was questioned by a man she believed to be Saint Priest, one of the king's ministers. When questioned, Rolin presented a simple interpretation of the women's purpose in Versailles. She said that they had come to apprise the king that "his good city of Paris" was lacking bread. The women waiting in the courtyard gave Chabry and Rolin a very negative reception. The group simply did not believe that the delegates had presented their case and obtained results. The king had apparently given the two women a paper on which was written his promise to see that the city of Paris received provisions. The women waiting outside thought that Chabry had received money from the king and that the papers she carried were not really signed by him. Rolin and Chabry were forced to show what was in their pockets in order to prove that they had not received money.[59] They were kicked and punched by the other women who also threatened to hang them.[60] Only the intervention of two bodyguards and two sympathetic women saved them. Rolin testified that after that she and Chabry went back into the king's apartments and he signed the papers.[61]

The king then appeared on the balcony with Chabry and supported her in her declaration that she had received no money. The papers were then given to one of the deputies who carried them back to the National Assembly, followed by the group of women. The seriousness of the women's intentions is obvious. Rolin and Chabry both returned to Paris late that evening in coaches supplied by the king. Louise Chabry testified that thirty-nine other women were in that group.[62] At about eight o'clock Mounier had returned with the deputation to the Assembly. He reported the words of the king and all the Assembly heard them and appeared to respect them. The king's only purpose, it was stated, was to "restore tranquillity among his people."[63]

Interestingly enough, several women claimed to have carried the king's decrees back to Paris. Madeleine Glain, a housekeeper from Paris, stated that she and two other women along with Maillard returned to the Hôtel de Ville in Paris and reported on the decrees that had been given to them at the National Assembly.[64] Louise Chabry maintained that she was in charge of a paper given to her by the king and that she had given it to the mayor upon her return to the city at two o'clock in the morning.[65] She may also have been part of Maillard's group.[66]

Many women, it appears, felt that the task had not yet been completed and that the promises made by the king were as yet far from reality. A large group remained in Versailles for the night and it was the actions of some of them that led to the notoriety of the events of October 6. Madame de la Tour du Pin reported that the women ate what had been found for them and then slept on the floor. According to her interpretation they were not all happy with the situation and some were crying, saying that they had been forced to march, and that they didn't know why they had come. This seems in most cases to have been highly unlikely because as we have seen the women's attitudes and actions pointed to goals that were well-defined. The leaders among the women slept in the National Assembly *pêle-mêle* with the deputies.[67]

Lafayette arrived in Versailles shortly before midnight with three contingents of the National Guard and a crowd of followers which included some women. He assured the king that although the National Guard supported the people of Paris in its efforts to obtain food, it would not stand by and see the royal family harmed. The next morning his words were put to the test. At about 6:30 a.m. a crowd of women entered the palace by way of an unguarded door, rushed up the stairs, and made their way to the apartments of the king and queen. One of the king's bodyguards, de Vallori, was killed immediately at the gate leading to the Cour des Princes. Another was killed a few minutes later after firing into the crowd and killing a young man, Jerome l'Heritier. Their heads were put on pikes for transport to Paris. Neither one was killed by women.

There can be little doubt that the chateau was inadequately guarded. Violence was not expected. The crowd numbered two hundred and the bodyguards could have fired but they did nothing. Only one Swiss guard appears to have been in place at the top of the marble staircase. Madame de la Tour du Pin lamented the sense of security which resulted in a lack of safety precautions against the possibility of the crowd turning violent.[68] Lafayette had placed around the chateau roughly the same number of guards as he would in peacetime and there were only about twenty of the king's bodyguards left in the vicinity. The rest had been sent to Trianon and Rambouillet. As the crowd poured up the staircase the bodyguards warned the queen and her ladies-in-waiting of the approaching danger. They managed to escape, seeking refuge in the apartments of the king.[69] A bodyguard of the king, François-Aimé de Miomandre de Sainte-Marie, testified at the Châtelet inquiry that he saw enter the chateau, by way of the Cour des Princes, "a crowd of people, armed with pikes, sticks, and other weapons." He described the violence and panic that followed as he made his way to the queen's apartment to warn her of the imminent danger.[70] Another witness, Elisabeth Girard, who had come with the women from Paris, testified that she had seen the brutal murder of one of the bodyguards.[71] Henriette-Adelaide Genet, lady-in-waiting to the queen, testified that she had heard at about 6:15 a.m. "a noise caused by women as they passed under the windows of the queen's apartment." Fifteen minutes later, she testified, the bodyguard, Miomandre, implored her to save the queen. She and another lady-in-waiting, Madame Thibault, helped the queen escape to the king's apartments and accompanied her there.[72] The king had in the meantime collected his children and returned to his apartment. The family then appeared together on the balcony. The National Guard managed to restore order and the crowd, in a sudden shift of mood, cheered the royal family.

Jeanne Martin Lavarenne, heroine of the Tuileries, was later to say that she spent the night at Versailles in the meeting room of the Assembly where, according to her and in direct contradiction of some accusations, nothing occurred "against honesty and decency." She and two other women made their way first of all to the Place d'Armes and then to the chateau. They were just in time to see the populace begin to assemble there. They witnessed the murder of two bodyguards and saw other bodyguards also threatened by the women. She reported that she was wounded by a blow to her right arm which she received while trying to divert a blow from a bodyguard. She described the attitude of the queen as she viewed the scene in the courtyard from the balcony. The queen, she said, was angry at what she witnessed. She felt betrayed and promised that she would never be fooled again. She promised to love her people and to be attached to them "as Jesus Christ is to his church."[73] The people heard their king, "his heart broken by sadness," agree to go to Paris. When he appeared on the balcony the crowd shouted, as if by inspiration, according to the witness, "The king to Paris! The king to Paris!" To this the king responded, "My children, you ask that I go to Paris, I will go; but on the condition that it will be with my wife and children."[74]

Preparations were soon underway and at about one p.m. the procession was ready to leave Versailles for Paris. The queen looked faint as she left the chateau to embark on the journey and she clutched at the robes of the king. One of the women shouted, "You have reason to hold on to the king; hold on tightly. He is your saviour."[75] Women constituted a good proportion of the crowd which accompanied the royal family. They carried branches of laurel. Next came the mounted National Guardsmen, numbering about one hundred. Behind them were the fusiliers and the grenadiers with the cannons between them. Intermingled with all these were the women, the bodyguards, and the soldiers of the Flanders regiment.[76] This group was followed by fifty to sixty wagons of grain and flour which were followed immediately by the carriages of the court. These were surrounded by deputies and cavalrymen and, of course, more women. Despite the diversity of the group and the triumphant attitude of the women, one witness claimed that the procession had more an atmosphere "of mourning and of sadness" than of celebration.[77] Bailly was to report, however, that the women, carrying the long branches of laurel, created a very picturesque effect among the rifles and the pikes. As they approached Paris, a woman pointed with one hand to the wagons of flour and with the other to the royal family. She supposedly said to the crowd lining the streets, "We are no longer lacking bread and we bring you the baker, the baker's wife, and the baker's son."[78]

The procession arrived in Paris at about eight o'clock in the evening. The city was lighted by lamps in windows in celebration of the king's return and the royal family was welcomed with cheers and shouts of approbation. Bailly presented the keys of the city to the king who accepted them and responded graciously to the mayor's welcoming address. "It is with pleasure and confidence always that I find myself in the midst of the citizens of my good city of Paris."[79] Bailly recounted later how he relayed this message incompletely to the audience, omitting the word "confidence" and how the queen and then the king corrected him.[80] After the official welcome accorded the family in the great hall of the Hôtel de Ville was finished and the crowd had responded with great applause, the royal family departed at about nine o'clock for the Tuileries. The crowd, including the women, dispersed for the night.

The women reappeared the next day at the Tuileries, demanding to see the queen. In an episode that is little known, they presented

« Vive le Roi ! Vive la Nation ! »
Estampe célébrant la journée du 7 octobre 1789.
Musée Carnavalet. (Photo F.A. Viollet)

"Long live the King! Long live the Nation!"
Celebration of the October Days. (Stamp) Courtesy Musée Carnavalet.

Marie Antoinette with their concerns. It is reported that the same women who, the evening before, had been mounted on the cannons and who had surrounded the carriage of the royal family on the trip to the capital, now stood on the terrace of the Tuileries below the queen's windows and demanded to see her. The queen appeared and she was told that it was time now that she distanced herself from the court and that she should now love the inhabitants of Paris. The queen responded that she had loved them at Versailles and that she would love them just the same in Paris. One woman in this crowd accused Marie Antoinette of having wished to bombard the city on 14 July and of hoping to flee the country on 6 October. The queen's response was to say that whoever had started these rumours was the perpetrator of the people's misfortune. When yet another one addressed her, and did so in German, the queen replied that "she had become so French that she had even forgotten her mother tongue." For this response she received applause and cheers from the group of women. The exchange ended when the queen gave ribbons and flowers from her hat to the women who cheered her with enthusiasm.[81] Of this meeting it was also said that women spoke to the queen with the same freedom as they would have spoken to anyone. They were neither more timid nor more bold than they had been before the Revolution.[82] Marie-Antoinette wrote on 7 October that the people had come to the Tuileries to request that the royal family remain in Paris. "I said to them, on behalf of the king, that it was out of my hands, that it depended on them and that we could ask for nothing better than to remain in Paris. All hate must cease and the least bloodshed would make us flee in horror. The one nearest me swore that all that was finished. I told the *poissardes* (market women who spoke the dialect called *poissarde*) to go and tell everything that we had just said."[83] Madame Tourzel, a lady-in-waiting to the queen, was later to say that the queen refused subsequently to comment on the events of those days. When the Commune of Paris, during its investigations, sent a deputation some days later to Marie-Antoinette, she refused to speak against the subjects of the king. Her reply to a deputation from the Châtelet was essentially the same. "I have seen all, known all, forgotten all."[84]

Who were the women who went to Versailles? This is a question which has proven very difficult to answer. The depositions given before the Châtelet inquiry provide some information, but opinions vary. Descriptions are so at variance that the only reasonable conclusion seems to be that almost every class was represented but the majority were of the working class, the female *sans-culotterie*. Some are described by contemporary sources as "higher than middle class" and "well-situated." Others are called *poissardes* and *canaille*.[85] One witness said that there were present very few who would be included in the category of "vile."[86] Mention is made of a woman, quite pretty, who had a sword in her hand and who marshalled the other women into action.[87] It is likely that this was Reine Audu, who is known to have been one of the leaders of the march and who was later imprisoned for her part in the events. It might also have been Théroigne de Méricourt who was living at Versailles that summer and who was present in the streets that day.[88] Each these women was an interesting revolutionary figure in her own right. Both were known to be street fighters and it is probable that they were present that day and participating in the activities.

Generally, it seems most likely that the crowd represented a cross

section of the population. Many of the women who were there testified later that they were forced to march. It was to their advantages,
of course, to deny enthusiastic participation and to thus avoid a jail
term. Almost none of the female witnesses at the Châtelet accepted
any responsibility at all for participating in the events of the October
Days. As noted previously Jeanne Martin Lavarenne insisted when
questioned that she had been forced to go.[89] Marie Pierre Louvain
Collinet testified that she had been taken, just like the others, by a
crowd of women to Versailles."[90] Françoise Miallou Carpentier testified that at about six o'clock in the morning as she was leaving
home she had been swept up by a crowd of women who were passing in the Rue Montorgueil and taken to Versailles.[91] Marie Catherine
Victoire Sacleux Némery testified that for three days it had been
impossible to obtain bread. She had heard that the women were going to the Hôtel de Ville for that purpose and she decided to join
them. Once there, the women determined that the wise thing to do
was to go to Versailles. This witness testified that she made it plain
that she did not wish to do that and had protested that she was not
wearing proper shoes and that she must return home. The women
refused to listen and she complained that she was made to pull one of
the three cannons all the way to Sèvres.[92] Catherine Potheau and
Anne Forêts gave identical testimonies, claiming that they had been
dragged by an immense crowd of women to Versailles. Even Louise
Chabry, star of the meeting with the king, maintained in her testimony that she had not wanted to go on the journey. She had been at
the Porte Saint Antoine with her parents that morning and she had
been forced, she said, by the "women of the people" to follow them
to Versailles. Françoise Rolin, Marguerite Paton, and Elisabeth Girard

all gave similar testimony. Paton said that she could not identify the women involved. Girard stated that the women threatened to cut off her hair. Jeanne-Dorothy Délaissement said that she was forced, like many other women, by the crowd who wished to go to Versailles.[93] None of the witnesses named a specific leader or group of instigators. Every witness, according to testimony, had been coerced by a group of nameless women. These testimonies contradict the enthusiastic participation witnessed on the actual march.

Some who went to Versailles that day, supposedly under duress, were middle class women. Françoise Miallou and Marie Pierre Louvain were merchants of toiletries and oysters, respectively. Women of the working class included Sacleux and Potheau, mentioned previously. Sacleux was a master fabric dyer and Potheau was a shop assistant, as was Anne Forêts. Louise Chabry, as previously mentioned, was a flower-seller. Madeleine Glain was a housekeeper and Jeanne Martin Lavarenne was a nurse. There were also porters of coal and of water. Some historians have claimed that there were prostitutes in the crowd but it seems that there is no evidence to support this.

Although many of the women who testified before the Châtelet appear to have been reasonably literate and articulate, there were many testimonies given there which recalled violent and vulgar threats against the queen. It becomes clear through the depositions that many of the women held the queen responsible for the political problems which the country faced and that any loyalty they might have felt for the king did not extend to her. One witness declared that he had been on the Rue Satory in Versailles at about seven p.m. on 5 October and he saw pass many *poissardes* and *femmes du peuple* (women of the

working class) whom, he said, "unleashed the most indecent proposals" against the queen. He testified that one of them had a knife in
her hand and said that she would be happy if she could open the
queen's stomach with it and tear out her heart.[94]   One of the king's
bodyguards testified that a woman in the crowd said to him, "It is not
bread that we ask, it is blood that is required. You are all beggars.
Your queen is a hussy, and we want her skin to make of it banners of
the districts."[95]   Another witness testified to the obscenities he had
heard with regard to the queen. He said that he had been asked by
some of the women where he was going and his response was that he
was following them and that he wondered where they were going.
They explained in obscene and graphic terms what their intentions
were and it was reported that this discourse was accompanied by
demonstrations. This witness added that each one of the women
wished to bring back something of Marie Antoinette. "[One] had
said that she would have a thigh; another said that she would have
the intestines." While saying these things they were dancing around
and holding out their aprons as if they had the desired body parts in
them.[96]   Anne-Marguerite Andelle testified that she was with a group
of women in the courtyard of the chateau at Versailles on October 5
who "vomited" accusations against the king and the queen and she
stated that these women accused the queen of having poisoned her
son, who had died the previous June, and of having dipped her hands
"in the blood of the French."[97]

A woman, seated in the small room which adjoined the Salle des
Menus Plaisirs, and reportedly drunk, was supposedly heard to say
that Marie Antoinette was solely responsible for the misfortunes of
the people.[98]   Another witness who had encountered the crowd on

the road between Sèvres and Viroflay testified that the people in the crowd, and particularly the women, swore that they would take the queen, dead or alive.[99] Elisabeth Girard in her testimony described the mayhem of the morning of 6 October and the murder of a bodyguard and said that during all this time she had heard abominable words spoken against the queen right up until the moment when the king had promised to go with his family to Paris. At that moment the trouble abated.[100] As well as exhibiting a threatening attitude to the queen, the women were less than enthusiastic about the presence of men on the journey. As the march began to take shape there were already comments of a negative nature being made about men attempting to join the group. The women complained of the men being weak and stated that they could make a better showing than the men in this time of strife. One witness who arrived at the Place de Grève on the morning of 5 October said that the Hôtel de Ville was occupied by a crowd of women who did not want any men among them.[101] In a letter written following the October Days, one woman expressed the opinion that during those days the women of Paris proved to the men that they were at least as brave as they were and just as enterprising. She stated that the history of that day had made her determined to make a very important motion in honor of women. In her words, "Let us send the men on their way, and let us not suffer with their systems of equality and of liberty, with their declarations of rights. They leave us in a state of inferiority, to tell the truth, in a state of slavery, in which they have held us for such a very long time."[102] Even Bailly said of the women gathered in the Place de Grève on the morning of 5 October that they were all shouting against the inclusion of men in their group.[103]

Lafayette led the National Guard to Versailles later in the day. They left Paris late in the afternoon and arrived at Versailles near midnight. It is Maillard's group, however, that is of interest here because such a large proportion of the participants were women. Accounts of contemporary journals confirm that women were in the majority and some journals attempted to estimate the size of the crowd. This has proven to be very difficult to do. *Le Courrier Français, Les Révolutions de Paris, Les annales Patriotiques et Littéraires* all estimated that the crowd numbered four to five thousand. *Le Journal de Versailles et Paris* stated that there were about three thousand in the group that marched. *L'Observateur* estimated that one thousand were present.[104] Estimates by individuals ran as low as four to five hundred.[105] Generally, however, it is agreed that the group was large and was composed mainly of women and that the men who were present played only a supporting role, just as the women had anticipated. Upon leaving Paris some of the women were heard to say that the men would be following and that they would help the women bring the king and queen to Paris.[106]

Historians have debated not only the size of the crowd but the question of whether or not the episode was planned in advance, instigated by the Duc d'Orléans, and carried out by his hirelings.[107] Although some witnesses at the Châtelet testified that some men of Orléans' entourage had been among the demonstrators and others said that some women were paid to go to Versailles it has never been shown definitively that there was such a plot involving this person.[108] Rather, the evidence points strongly to an uprising of a spontaneous nature. Few if any of the women who assembled on the morning of 5 October at the Place de Grève had been paid to do so. Judging from the testimony at the Châtelet and from eye-witness accounts, they came from all walks of life in response to the call from the streets. The oft-repeated claim of forced participation is easy to understand in the circumstances of the Châtelet inquiry. Imprisonment was the fate of those women who had an enthusiastically high profile during the action; too high, that is, to support any subsequent denial. One such person was Reine Audu, who made her reputation as a street activist during the October Days. After the Châtelet inquiry she spent almost a year in prison. The women on the march were for the most part unprepared for the journey. Some had not eaten for many hours and were without money. However, as testimony has shown, even in this condition there were present many who were enthusiastic participants with a penchant for political slogans and who demonstrated a great desire to see their king at Versailles and to bring him to Paris. Testimony claiming that there were men dressed as women in the crowd undeniably exists and is often used in support of the Orleanist plot theory. There is evidence, however, that shows that these men were not at the Place de Grève until much later in the day on 5 October, long after the women's activity was underway.[109]

That the October Days were primarily days of political expression and political growth for women is borne out by the testimonies of Marie Rose Bare, Louise Chabry, and Françoise Rolin. Their words demonsrate that they had made the connection in their thinking between the immediate shortage of bread in the capital and the shortcomings of the existing political system, and also bear witness to the truth of the statement that "they wanted bread but not at the price of liberty."[110] The depositions given at the Châtelet illustrate the greatly expanded role that women played once they had reached Versailles. Their simple goal of alleviating the shortage of food was transformed into a political involvement with more than one dimension. The issue of bread spurred the women to action and brought about the gathering of the female crowd, but they were still very much aware of other realities as well. They went on to voice complaints in the Assembly about the abuse of the highly symbolic cockade and to complain that the promulgation of the Constitution was being delayed by the clergy. Their performance there, although so effective that one of the deputies suggested, in all seriousness, that the women should be allowed to vote with the deputies,[111] was only the beginning. It was at the meeting with the king that the individual women shone. Demonstrating an unexpected sophistication and preparation, they conversed with the king and ministers of the king in a quite astonishing manner. Keeping in mind that these were women of the people mixed with some from the bourgeoisie and also realizing the reverence with which the people regarded royalty, their ability to present their concerns was truly surprising. It is certain that they had not only made the connection in their minds between the shortage of bread in the capital and the existing political system, but also that they possessed sensibilities and understanding in a political sense that reached far beyond any objective that had thus far been articulated. Marie Rose Bare, a lace worker, testified that on 5 October at about eight o'clock she had been stopped on her way to work by a group of about a hundred women who insisted that she must go with them to ask for bread. She also described a much larger role that she played once the group was at Versailles. The women obviously presented their case very well during their audience with the king and they were well able to carry on a conversation with Saint-Priest, one of the king's ministers who was in the king's ante-chamber at the time.[112] Bare tesified that the women complained to the king about the shortage of bread and that the king responded that he suffered as much as they did to see that they did not have it. The women went on to explain to the king that the convoys carrying flour to Paris needed an escort because they had been told that of sixty-six wagons destined for Paris only two had actually arrived. The results were immediate and quite dramatic. The king promised to give the wagons an escort and he stated that if it were up to him, the women would have bread immediately.[113] There were other women as well who met with the king and whose testimonies show that they were well able to deal with the situation. Once at Versailles they very ably confronted the king with their specific grievances and expressed specific political concerns during the encounter. They knew exactly why they were there and exactly what they wanted and they had no problem in articulating their concerns. Even Louise Chabry, the seventeen-year-old flower seller who fainted in the presence of the king, was nevertheless able to express her grievances. She knew exactly why she was at Versailles. She said that she had had the honour of carrying the complaints of the women and of the people to the king. She was there to ask for bread and for the necessities of life. Françoise Rolin gave much the same description of her objectives.[114] She stated that the women had come to Versailles to inform the king that Paris lacked bread. When questioned further by some of the king's ministers she was able to explain that the women had attempted to make the same demand in Paris but there was no one at the Hôtel de Ville. Rolin, like Chabry and Bare, demonstrated that she was highly aware of her purpose in Versailles and that she understood and was able to communicate the need for political intervention.

Another major goal, this one highly political in nature, that the women had articulated from the time they left Paris and even before, was that of bringing the king back to the capital so that he would reside at the Louvre among his subjects. They felt that if he were there, closer to his people than he could be at Versailles, their government and therefore their lives would be greatly improved. Also they would be able to watch closely over his activities. When the royal family appeared on the balcony on the morning of 6 October the cry went up from the crowd "The king to Paris!" The next day, after the royal family was settled in the palace of the Tuileries, Marat wrote in his journal that having finally brought the king to Paris was an occasion for the good Parisians to celebrate. The king's presence, Marat said, would make a great difference and the people would no longer die of hunger. As for the king, "He shares the joy of his dear citizens."[115] Françoise Rolin recounted that once back at the National Assembly she and some other women had declared that it was their wish that the king should come to Paris because there he would have a better understanding of what was happening and things would go much better. At this point, she said, one of the men present told her to keep quiet, that she did not know what she was asking.[116] Such evidence demonstrated that the men felt threatened when the women made political statements of this type. The testimony of Madeleine Glain is interesting as well because it shows the presence of a political awareness that is often not recognized. She testified that although she was forced to march she made a good account of herself once at Versailles. She was chosen to meet with the king, proceeded to communicate with him on the topic of lack of necessities in Paris, carried the decrees of the king back to the Hôtel de Ville in Paris, and then went to the Oratoire district to impart the news that the king had signed the decrees and had promised to safeguard the provisioning of the city. This was a role of no small importance for someone who had supposedly gone unexpectedly to Versailles and was therefore totally unprepared for what might happen there. Madeleine Glain demonstrated a good deal of awareness in her performance during the October Days which negates the possibility of total political ignorance or mere chance.

It can be said after careful study of the roles of these and other female participants that although they attempted to minimize the importance of their activities, claimed that they had been forced to go to Versailles, and tried to camouflage details of their intrusion into the National Assembly, there can be little doubt that the women were indeed active and enthusiastic participants in the October Days. They were in fact credited with having liberated France.

> Providence alone has saved us and by the most feeble means in order that we derived all the glory. It has inspired in the women the resolution to free the *patrie* (native land) and it has made them succeed. They have obtained from the king [the promise] that he will live amongst us and nothing more is necessary.[117]

The women were insisting on new roles within the new nation and took seriously the possibilities presented by the changing times. They were determined that the king should listen to their grievances and demands. They masked the facts of their participation for obvious reasons when they were later questioned at the Châtelet inquiry. Their actions belie their words, however, and show that the women were willing and informed political participants, and although this participation was still in its fledgling form, there can be little doubt that they were heading in the direction of a wider involvement in the revolutionary arena.

CHAPTER TWO

WOMEN AND REVOLUTIONARY POLITICS

... les femmes, renfermées toute leur vie dans le cercle d'un petit nombre de connaissances frivoles, sont les premières victimes de l'ignorance; faiblesse, sensibilité, delicatesse, telle est leur nature. (...women, enclosed all their lives in a circle of frivolous acquaintances, are the first victims of ignorance; weak, sensitive, fragile, such is their nature.) President Grandchamp in the *Journal de la Société Populaire des amis de la constitution établié à Lyon.*

Women and the Clubs

After the women brought the king to Paris on October 6, 1789, the National Assembly soon followed. It established itself in the Salle de Manège, where it proceeded to carry out its self-ordained task of formulating a constitution for France. A sense of calm settled over the country, buttressed by the wider availability of bread and a decline in prices. After the months of crisis, the insurgents of 1789, women as well as men, returned to their more normal ways of life. But the political ferment of 1789 continued to find expression at all levels of society, and in various forms. One was the series of mass public demonstrations, or *fêtes,* celebrating notable dates and themes of the Revolution, in which women participated along with the men. Perhaps the most famous of these was the *Fête de la Federation* at the Champ de Mars in Paris on 14 July, 1790, the first anniversary of the capture of the Bastille; contemporary illustrations of the scene include many women among the thousands of participants. And among the many new images reflecting

the revolutionary fervor, the female figure of "Liberty" soon became
a predominant symbol.[1]   Another more practical and continuing form
of political activity involving women was the organization of a great
number and variety of political and "popular" societies and clubs.
Most of these organizations, like the National Assembly itself and
the Breton Club, ancestor of the Jacobins, were at first exclusively
male in membership. Soon, however, women began to appear as
spectators in clubs such as the Cordeliers and the Jacobins in Paris.
It was in these surroundings that much of the women's political growth
was to take place. From the beginning the *Société des Cordeliers*
allowed women to observe and even to speak, but not to vote. However, some clubs soon opened their membership to women as well as
to men and as early as 1789 a few clubs made up exclusively of
women began to appear.

Paris was naturally the centre of this "mixed" and female club
activity but important clubs were also organized in Lyon and in many
other provincial towns. Historians have identified more than thirty
women's political clubs in cities such as Lyon, Dijon, and Bordeaux
(though not Marseille), and in many other places scattered throughout France, with a concentration for reasons as yet unexplained in
the southwest, in towns such as Bayonne, Pau, Montauban and
Damazan.[2]

In January, 1790, in Paris, Théroigne de Méricourt founded the
short-lived *Amis de la Loi*, a fraternal society which was to allow
both men and women to actively participate. The purpose would be
to enlighten the populace in political matters and to dispel fear and
ignorance.[3]   Although the society did not last long, de Méricourt
managed to address a meeting of the Cordeliers Club in February of

that year with a proposal that a new building be constructed to house the National Assembly in a good deal more grandeur than the Manège provided.[4]   Although her suggestion did not live to see the light of day, the action is noteworthy in that a woman made such an address at that time.

November of 1790 witnessed the beginnings of the mixed club in Paris. Claude Dansard, who ran a boarding house in Paris, at first organized meetings in a room at the Jacobin monastery for artisans and fruit and vegetable merchants, some of who attended accompanied by their wives and children. The principal purpose of the meetings was to read and discuss decrees of the National Assembly.[5] The gatherings provided the women with a true political setting. In March of 1791 this group took the name of *Société Fraternelle de Patriotes des Deux Sexes*. This particular organization soon increased rapidly in respect to both its membership and popularity and other fraternal societies proliferated in Paris in the months that followed. One of the first was the *Société Populaire de Mauconseil* which later took the name of *Société Fraternelle des Halles* when it moved its meetings to that quarter. There were also the *Société Fraternelle des Minimes* and that of *Nomophiles* , both founded in the early months of 1791. These met in the section of the Palais Royal. Prudhomme, the anti-female editor of *Révolutions de Paris*, established the *Société des Indigents* which accepted women as members. His actions there belied the thrust of his journal, for he had his wife preside. At about the same time the *Société Fraternelle des Amis des Droits del'Homme Ennemie du Despotisme* was established. In 1792 the *Société Fraternelle de Sainte-Geneviève* became the *Société Fraternelle des Deux Sexes du Panthéon-Français.*[6]   It was in these clubs which welcomed women as members that the basis was established for the process of their politicization. Here in the popular fraternal societies many women took their first steps toward becoming vocal and informed participants in the new social and political order.

The role of women in the *Société Fraternelle des Deux Sexes,* which met at the Jacobin convent on Rue Saint-Honoré is the one for which most information is available. According to *Babillard,* the journal of the Abbé Fauchet's *Cercle Social,* the women were participating at the same level as the men in both discussions and elections.[7] Two women acted as secretaries. Their duties included the examination of the lists of the aspiring members and the organization of their introductions into the society. Four men fulfilled the same function for their sex and a secretary for each group, male and female, was seated on either side of the president. The women were able, like the men, to present all the hopeful candidates on their lists. The women participated on an equal footing with the men in this matter. A committee of twelve persons, six men and six women, comprised a conciliation committee which examined issues and settled disputes. As well, women made up part of the delegations and commissions of the organization.[8] Although there is no evidence that any ever succeeded, it seems that women even aspired to the presidency. *Babillard* reported that a woman confronted the members with such a request. "What difference is there between the men and us? I ask that we be allowed to be named not only to the secretariat and the commissariat, but to the presidency as well." It was reported that the speaker was pretty so some applauded. One member was said to have complained that this acceptance of women was the perfect way to assure the dissolution of the society.[9]

The preamble to the club's regulations stated that ignorance and suspicion of the laws of the land would bring about the destruction of liberty and the work of the Revolution generally. The most formidable obstacle to the enemies of the nation would be in the strength of the friends of the constitution who shared a love of liberty and equality and who would participate in peaceful discussion of the public good, believing that the people always have the right to demand administrative accountability in matters of government.[10] This attitude is similar to that expressed by Robespierre and Brissot who protested the proscription of political participation of passive citizens, a category which included all women as well as the poorer men who were members of the popular societies.[11]

There were thirty-nine articles in the original Règlement and two more were added later. The participation of women was ensured in the articles which delineated their functions. Article II stated that "all members of the two sexes will participate in the deliberations and in the discussions." Article V made provision for two elected secretaries who would keep track of the names of "sisters" who wished to be admitted to the society. In elections there would be six scrutineers drawn from the two sexes. Article X made clear that admission requirements applied equally to both sexes, stating that all those wishing to be admitted to the society must be supported by two "brothers" or "sisters." The registration procedure for new members always referred to "brothers" and "sisters." Article XII declared that any brother or sister, newly received into the society, would be called upon by the president, in the name of the society, to take the civic oath, as follows:

> I swear to be faithful to the nation, to the law, and to the king, and to support French liberty with all my strength, and the rights of man and citizen as well. I promise to be faithful to the rules of the society, as long as it exists.[12]

The organization was obviously political in its direction and one of its priorities was to provide a political education for its members, both male and female.

Among the members of the *Société Fraternelle des Deux Sexes*, one female member particularly stands out due to her dedication and involvement. The political education of women was one of the main concerns of Louise Keralio, later Louise Robert, who had begun publishing the *Mercure nationale ou Journal d'Etat et du Citoyen* in August, 1789. She was not limited in her vision of female participation to the modest role allowed women in the fraternal societies but aspired to larger things. She envisioned a humanitarian role for women in the clubs which would involve an active participation in improving the lot of the unfortunate. She proposed a system of hospital visits during which society members would evaluate and report on their observations to the Directory of the Department, to the municipality of Paris, to the forty-eight sections, and to all the patriotic societies of the realm. This would be delivered together with an invitation to accord the information "the greatest consideration."[13]

It was not long before fears that the popular societies might become too powerful began to surface. A pamphlet entitled *Avis aux Français sur les clubs* warned of the dangers of allowing the clubs to wield so much influence.

> Everywhere they are organizing clubs....The enthusiasm for clubs takes over all
> classes, all ages, all sexes. Artisans leave their work in order to talk nonsense in
> the clubs. In other places one sees young girls sacrificed to the frenzy of the day.
> Besides this, the women themselves form clubs where they learn to worship the
> idol of fanaticism....The entire country will soon be only a club.[14]

In the spring of 1791 the idea of associating all the fraternal societies under the umbrella of the Cordeliers was born.[15] In May the
Comité Central des Sociétés Fraternelles was created with François
Robert, husband of Louise Keralio Robert, as president. From that
day forward the women of the clubs were involved in a highly energetic and tenacious political movement which was to grow in strength
and determination as the Revolution progressed.

Generally, the fraternal clubs in both Paris and the provinces were
concerned with a variety of activities which illustrated the growth of
political awareness and dedication to political causes on the part of
women. Their civic consciousness was illustrated by their enthusiastic participation in many *fêtes* and they showed a concern for public welfare (particularly after the war against Austria began in April,
1792), an interest in civic instruction based on the idea that every
individual must serve the nation as her first responsibility, and a concern for the education of young girls. Several times women claimed
the right to bear arms for the nation. Pauline Léon appeared before
the Legislative Assembly in March of 1792 with a petition signed by
more than three hundred women of the *Société Fraternelle des
Minimes* demanding the right to arm themselves for defense. The
petition stated that the women's purpose was not to abandon the care
of families and homes, but simply to be able to defend themselves. It
queried whether women should allow themselves to be slaughtered

without having the right to defend themselves. In case the enemy was victorious, would it not be cruel to condemn women to wait, unarmed, in their houses for a terrible death, accompanied by all the horrors which would no doubt precede it or perhaps to experience a worse horror yet, that of surviving when all that they held dear, such as family and liberty, had been destroyed.[16] Only a few days later, Théroigne de Méricourt, member of the *Société Fraternelle des Deux Sexes* proposed to the women of the Faubourg Saint-Antoine that a legion of armed women be formed. She reminded the women at the meeting of the *Société Fraternelle des Minimes* that as women they were constantly in danger and stated that "we owe all to the *patrie*." The women must exhibit unity and fraternity and be wise and calm in their efforts. "We must prepare with as much wisdom as courage to repulse the attacks of our enemies. We must arm ourselves. We have that right, by nature and even by law." She stated that women must show men that they are their equals in both courage and virtue. "We will show all of Europe that the French know their rights and are at the height of eighteenth century enlightenment."[17] She went on to encourage women to fight at the sides of their men in order to repulse the enemies of liberty.[18]

Meanwhile, in the provinces, the women were also in the process of organizing themselves for more effective participation. In 1789 in Dijon the women had founded the *Club des Femmes de Dijon*. At Breteuil the young women had organized the *Sœurs de la Constitution* in August of 1790. Its regulation by civic authorities was strict. The mayor was to observe the meetings, but could act only as a consultant. At Aunay the women organized in the *Légion des Amazones* and remained undaunted in the face of opposition from soldiers and aristocrats. During the summer of 1791, the women of Bordeaux, three or four thousand strong, organized themselves into the *Société des Amies de la Constitution* and marched in a procession to present a bouquet to the constitutional bishop of Bordeaux. It was reported that this triumphal march, escorted by national troops and soldiers of Agénois, was a great spectacle, of an "august character," inspiring respect and tenderness and recalling to the imagination the celebrations of the Greeks which modern religions had lost.[19] At Tours the same summer six hundred women planned a procession to the Champ de Mars. A group of women would march in two lines with all mothers in the line on the right. It was decided that the headgear would be a *pouf* of white net, to which would be attached a cockade of ribbons in the national colours. Hair would be arranged in chignons. The uniform would be white with a green ribbon running down the side.[20]

It was not long before the women of Paris, having done apprenticeship in the fraternal societies, were also responding with enthusiasm to the call for clubs that were uniquely female in membership. In these all-female assemblies the education of women was to continue. The object there would be, as in the fraternal societies, to raise the political awareness of the membership. Although only two such clubs were to emerge in Paris, each was of importance in its own right. First came the *Société Patriotique et Bienfaisance des Amies de la Vérité* (March 1791) and later came the *Société des Citoyennes Républicaines Révolutionnaires* (May, 1793).

The first of these was an offshoot of the Abbé Fauchet's *Cercle Social* which was founded at the Palais Royal in the autumn of 1790. Here he preached to a group that was largely composed of women, although it was officially a fraternal society. Later that year, in December, Etta Palm d'Aelders gave an address there in which she encouraged the women to take action in the public arena. Entitled *Discours sur l'injustice des lois en faveur des hommes au depens des femmes,* her speech deplored the type of woman who gave herself over totally to the duties of household and family. She felt that women had been sacrificed to all the prejudices, subjected early in life to the wills of their fathers and later to the whims of their husbands. She felt that women were "victims of an education that took away their courage and suffocated their spirits."[21] Furthermore, she advocated that since the French had descended from the Romans the women should now imitate the Roman women in courage and determination.[22] It is not surprising that she should call shortly thereafter for popular societies composed of a strictly female membership. The following spring Palm d'Aelders founded the *Sociéte Patriotique et de Bienfaisance des Amies de la Verité.* In March, 1791, she requested that there be created in every section of the capital women's clubs which would enter into communication with all the fraternal societies of France. *Les Amies de la Vérité* would oversee their activities and the heads of the assemblies would meet, under the supervision of *Les Amies*, every week in a *Directoire genérale.* These clubs would have a humanitarian as well as a political purpose. Their worthy goals were to be carried out within the context of a growing political understanding of the new *nation.* Members would help the indigent, visit the sick, and watch over the education and nutrition of children.[23]

Enthusiastic women gathered at the offices of the *Cercle Social* at five o'clock on 25 March, 1791 for the first meeting of the group. The birth of this first uniquely female club in Paris did not go unnoticed. In the *Patriote Français* on April 1, the editor, Brissot de Warville, commented on the formation of the patriotic clubs at Bordeaux, Alais, and Nantes and he added that Paris would do well to possess such a useful institution as a patriotique club.[24]   About this same time, Palm d'Aelders, as president of *Les Amies* gave a rousing speech to the men of the *Cercle Social.* She proclaimed that nature had created woman to be man's companion in his work and in his glory. She stated that woman had been created the equal of man in moral strength and was created his superior in vivacity of imagination, sensitivity, strength in adversity, patience during suffering, and finally, in generosity of soul and in patriotic zeal.[25]

In May, this same firebrand managed to receive permission from the Consituent Assembly for her group to hold meetings in one of the vacant convents in Paris. On the twenty-second of May her request for protection and support for the club was presented to the Directory of the department.[26]   She then directed an address to the forty-eight sections to inform the people of the club's main objectives, in accordance with the broader goals of the Revolution. In the interests of liberty, humanity, and equality she wished to form an institution to raise and educate young girls born into indigent families so that they could earn an honest living as adults. She asked that each section name two women to participate by disseminating their knowledge and contributing three *livres* per month. Not one section appears to have responded. Not easily discouraged, *Les Amies* had a prospectus printed which they distributed widely in Paris. This brochure especially targeted the bishops and the *curés* and all persons known to be wealthy. It described the society's goals as follows:

> In the new order of things which we owe to Liberty, each individual can and must serve the Nation. Old people, women, children, none are without the means to serve; it is necessary only to develop these means, to employ them appropriately, and to replace destructive prejudices with regenerative virtues.[27]

Again the club received virtually no response with the exception of a magistrate who donated one hundred *livres*. The club had mainly only the contributions of its members and after expenses it was left with only seven hundred *livres* to carry out its worthy objectives.[28] In April 1792, the society appealed once more for funds to give a second opportunity to those who regretted not having responded before. The response was as usual. The membership fee was very high for the time and this indicates that the women who could afford to belong to the club were mainly *bourgeoises*. Their poorer sisters, for whom they showed much concern and on whose behalf they were prepared to work diligently, obviously could not have afforded the dues. The club dissolved sometime during the autumn months of 1792 and Palm d'Aelders left France in November and took up residence in Holland.[29]

Women's activities entered a different phase after the king accepted the new Constitution in September of 1791. Despite their contributions to the cause of the Revolution during the October Days and afterwards, there had been no serious attempt to enfranchise women by the Constituent Assembly, and women had no political rights in the new sustem. In the very month in which the new Constitution went into effect, however, Olympe de Gouges demanded these rights in her historic Declaration of the Rights of Women. The pamphlet

had very little impact at the time.[30]   During the period of the Legislative Assembly, some of the mixed and women's clubs continued to
meet, and women also occasionally presented addresses to the Assembly or joined with crowds of men in presenting petitions on various occasions. On 19 October, 1791, for example, a market woman
presented an address in which she declared, "Thanks to the patriotic
deputies, France is beginning to enjoy liberty, but the main work is
not complete." She then declared that the people of France had placed
their fate in the hands of the deputies who were the sole hope of the
people and that the people had made a "wise and considered choice"
when they put their faith in these men. The people hoped that the
Constitution of the realm would be "the most beautiful work of
mortals."[31]

On April 1, 1792 Palm d'Aelders had presented to the Assembly a
petition in which she asked the deputies to take under consideration
the state of degradation to which women were reduced in the matter
of political rights and to reclaim for them "the full enjoyment of
natural rights of which they have been deprived by a long repression." Men, she declared, were finally free. Women, however, were
"slaves of a thousand prejudices." Therefore, she was requesting
that the Assembly give to females the right to a "moral education"
and that they declare them adults at age twenty-one. As well, she
asked that political liberty and equality of rights be granted to both
sexes and that a divorce law be passed. The presiding deputy responded vaguely that "the Assembly would avoid, in the laws that it
is entrusted to make, all that would excite their regrets and their
tears."[32]   Indeed, the Assembly later in the year did grant women
legal majority at the age of twenty-one, including the right to appear

as witnesses in civil lawsuits, and produced a law making divorce possible by mutual consent or marital incompatibility.[33]

In addition, the period of the Constituent and Legislative Assemblies also witnessed the appearance of a number of newspapers published by women's groups and edited by women or addressed to a female audience, particularly in Paris.[34]   One such journal complained, "We suffer more than men, who with their declarations of rights, leave us in a state of inferiority," and went on to suggest that there should be female representatives at the National Assembly.[35] There were other journals published by women that were little known.[36]   Some were even written by men.   One of these was *L'Observateur feminin*   and this one made fun of Théroigne de Méricourt.[37]   Later there appeared several periodicals addressed to women bearing a title reminiscent of very popular periodicals produced for working-class men of Paris, *Mère Duchesne.*[38]

The major event of early 1792 was the declaration of war against Austria. This followed months of debate both within the Legislative Assembly and the clubs, in particular the Paris Jacobin club which heard heated exchanges between two of its most prominent members, Brissot and Robespierre. Some women, as noted previously, advocated that legions of amazons be formed, but little came of these suggestions. It was in 1792 that Madame Roland began her remarkable political career after her husband became Minister of the Interior in the first "patriot" or Girondin ministry which was created in March.[39]   The summer of 1792 also witnessed two more insurrections, those of June 20 and August 10, and women played at least a supporting role in both of these. The invasion of the Tuileries Palace on June 20 was led by *sans-culottes* of the Faubourg Saint-Antoine;

although not even George Rudé was able to find much precise information about the insurgents, he does note that they included some women.[40] In the much more significant insurrection of August 10, which overthrew the monarchy, three women not only played active roles, but were formally decorated for their efforts with civic crowns from the Commune of Paris. The three were Reine Audu, Théroigne de Méricourt, and Claire Lacombe, who later became president of the most active and most famous of the women's clubs, *Les Citoyennes Républicaines Révolutionnaires.* Although she was not decorated, a fourth woman, Pauline Léon, also was among the insurgents of August 10.

The fall of the monarchy also brought an end to the Legislative Assembly and to the entire constitutional edifice of 1791, and opened the period of the National Convention and the Republic, the most radical phase of the Revolution and the one in which women's organized political participation was to reach its zenith.

OLYMPE DE GOUGES AND THÉROIGNE DE MÉRICOURT

It seems appropriate to discuss tthe lives and careers of one or two of the women involved in revolutionary activities in some detail. Participants in demonstrations, insurrections, and club organizations included a number of outstanding individuals, all of who qualified as revolutionaries. Each one, however, possessed a unique personal history and operated within the revolutionary context with very specific motivations, attitudes, and interests. Two such individuals were Olympe de Gouges and Théroigne de Méricourt; the first wrote commentary on the Revolution and the second participated as a street activist.

Olympe de Gouges has been called by a French historian "the great unknown revolutionary of our history."[41]   Known or unknown, she deserves recognition and a place in history because of her advanced political ideas, her views on the position of women in society, and her general critique of societal attitudes and human institutions. It must be admitted that although her name is remembered, the extent of her ideas and activities has remained largely unexplored. Her female perspective was reflected in her political commentary. As revolutionary scribe she dealt with many of the important themes and events of the period, using a variety of techniques in her written responses to emerging situations.

In the years preceding the Revolution, she concentrated on themes of social justice which later gave way to works of political and religious nature. Many were written in response to specific events and trace the path of her changing political loyalties. In July, 1789 she was an ardent revolutionary who supported the attack on the Bastille and cheered the people's victory. The following October she expressed sympathy for the monarchy and condemned the perpetrators of the king's embarrassment and return to Paris. In June of 1791, at the time of the king's flight to Varennes, she was a staunch republican, but at the time of the king's trial, in December, 1792, she offered to defend him.

In summary, de Gouges' enthusiastic, if somewhat unstable, response to the Revolution resulted from her belief that society was corrupt and that women particularly were the victims of oppression and injustice. Her hope for mankind lay with revolutionary reform. Women, she stated, were excluded from all power and knowledge.[42]

Her response to the convocation of the Estates-General was *Le Cri du Sage* in which she exhorted women to take action and improve their attitudes saying that they were at the same time feeble and all-powerful, the betrayed and the betrayer. She went on to express her views regarding the problems confronting the Estates-General. She felt that if virtue and patriotism did exist they should already be making themselves felt there. If this were indeed the case the three orders together would only be able to decide "in favour of the public wellbeing." She warned against a spirit of discord. The nobility, she said, must be convinced that it was an injustice to refuse to sit with the Third Estate "as if there were between these two orders insurmountable barriers." She stated her political aspirations as follows:

> I wish that the king reascend his throne, that the nation recognize that his descent from it is the misfortune of France, that the French, leaving aside the sabre and the cartridge pouch, reunite at the head of their affairs.[43]

De Gouges continued to write on a variety of topics and in September of 1791 she produced the work for which she is best remembered. It was entitled *Declaration of the Rights of Woman and Citizeness, dedicated to the Queen.* In the opening lines of the preface she informed the queen that she had not waited for liberty to reign before she expressed her opinions. She stated that she had always been involved even at a time when it was dangerous to do so because "the blindness of despots punished such noble audacity." She explained to the queen that she had always defended her even when others spoke against her. She thought it important that the queen take the part of women and she felt that the Revolution could only succeed if women were freed from their deplorable state. She wished to set before all members of society a declaration of the natural, inalienable, and sacred rights of women in a way that would constantly remind them of their rights and obligations. She wished that the claims of the citizenesses, founded on simple inarguable principles, would work always to maintain the Constitution, good morals, and the happiness of all.[44]

She maintained that women were born free and equal to men in their rights. She claimed for each one the "natural and inalienable" rights of liberty, property, security, and especially resistance to oppression (Article II). She stated that the natural rights of women had been limited by men's perpetual tyranny and this must be remedied by the laws of nature and of reason which, in their wisdom, proscribe all acts harmful to society (Article IV). The next four articles deal with the general will and equality of opportunity according to capability, the equality of women before the law, the application of established law to women in a just manner. Article X is the one that has inspired the most comment. "Woman," she said, "has the right to mount the scaffold. She must have equally the right to mount the tribune." Historians have observed that as things turned out she was accorded only the first of these. The last article dealt with property. It stated that it belonged to both sexes, whether united or separate, and that it is for each sacred and inviolable. The only possible reason for depriving a person of property would be if the public need, legally determined, dictated it and then only on the condition of a fair and previous indemnity.

Throughout the period of the Legislative Assembly de Gouges grew increasingly suspicious of the motives and activities of the Jacobins. She referred to their club as a "hideaway for reprobates" and as a "den of thieves." She spoke out against the uprising of 20 June, 1792[45] but in the autumn of the same year, after the bloody September massacres, she expressed the belief that there could no longer be a reconciliation between monarchical principles and the new republican sentiments.[46] During the same autumn she responded to the events of 10 August in a letter to King Frederick William II of Prussia and she advised him to withdraw his armies from French territory immediately. This epistle marked the end of her support for the monarchy.[47]

The attitude of the French press toward de Gouges as expressed during the summer and autumn of 1792 was negative. After her participation in a procession on July 14, accompanied, among others, by Théroigne de Méricourt and Etta Palm d'Aelders, the royalist *Tableau de Paris* described them as being "a choir of national virgins just as extravagant as they are ridiculous." *Révolutions de Paris* commented that de Gouges was merely showing off.[48] The same autumn (1792) she expressed openly and emphatically her dislike for many of the Jacobin leaders. Marat she regarded as "a destroyer of laws, mortal enemy of order, of humanity, and of his country." She accused him of living at liberty in a society in which he was both a tyrant and a plague.[49] She also made written comment on Robespierre, portraying him as essentially evil and making a chilling prediction which expressed her sympathy with the Girondins in their acceleraing conflict with the Mountain in the Assembly. "You wish to assassinate Pétion, Roland, Vergniaud, Condorcet, Louvet, Brissot, Lasource, Guadet, Gensonné, Hérault de Séchelles; in a word, all the flames of the Republic and of patriotism."[50] Of this group only Louvet was to survive the Terror.

In yet another attack she suggested that she and Robespierre drown themselves together in the Seine. She said that Robespierre had stated that he would give his life for the glory of his country but had delivered only the "greatest of plagues." She felt that there was no better way she could serve her country than to give her life in order to get rid of him. Her comments did not go unnoticed and members of the Jacobin Club expressed concern. Her response was swift and she denied all accusations and made derogatory comments about the lack of participation of certain Jacobins at the beginning of the Revolution.[51]

One month before the execution of the king, de Gouges wrote a letter to the Convention asking that his life be spared. She said that he would be taking the punishment for his ancestors. She questioned whether he was more guilty or dangerous than his brothers or his son. She concluded that it is not sufficient simply to behead a king in order to kill him. He can survive for a long time afterward. On the other hand he can survive his fall but be truly dead.[52] One of the deputies is reported to have offered twenty-four *sous* for her head to which she responded that it was worth at least thirty. Being both witty and quick-witted, she escaped severe punishment, at least for a time. *Les Révolutions de Paris* responded to the incident by saying that de Gouges would do better to knit pantelons for the *sans-culottes* and went on to challenge its readership to imagine the results if there were two hundred more like her seated in the Convention next to the Abbé Fauchet.[53] Later, in her pamphlet *Avis pressant à la Convention, par une vraie Républicaine,* she said, "It is my opinion that any true Republican will not vote for his [the king's] death....The greatest crime of Louis Capet was to have been born in a time when philosophy was silently preparing the foundations of the Republic."[54]

Two days after the execution of the king on 21 January, de Gouges' play *L'Entrée du Dumouriez à Bruxelles* opened at the Théâtre de la République (Comédie Française). The play depicted the French in their role as liberators of other European nations and the author wished to show that the French destroyed tyrants but not their subjects. One of her characters delivered the argument to the vanquished that "the French are your friends; they wish only to destroy tyrants in order to free nations; they have begun with their own; imitate them; the soldiers are all brothers and must unite for the universal cause of peoples."[55] Although the content was revolutionary, the play was not well received. Perhaps de Gouges recent intervention on the side of the king rendered the audience less than responsive. On opening night spectators demanded the playwright, who was chased from the theatre with members of the audience in hot pursuit. Not one to let such an event go without comment, de Gouges responded in the days which followed with yet another poster and defended her position. In this one, *Complots dévoilés,* she said that the wretches accused her of being unpatriotic because she had defended the king and because she thought that his death was useless and would become fatal to the Republic.[56]

' When she wrote *Avis pressant à la Convention, par une vraie Républicaine* in April, 1793, she proceeded to post it around Paris, as was her usual custom. In it she condemned the growing dissension among the factions in the Convention, saying that the factions were playing right into the hands of the aristocrats who had been heard to say that the fools in the Convention were no longer getting along and therefore their (the aristocrats') triumph was a certainty.[57]

On June 4, 1793 de Gouges wrote her *Testament Politique* and addressed it to the Jacobins, the Commune and the forty-eight sections of Paris. In it she deplored the actions of the Convention during the preceding days when the Girondins had been expelled. She accused the Jacobins of thinking that France could be saved merely by the *grande proscription*. To the Girondins, whom she called the "noble victims of the 31 May," she said that "it is in the same death that you await that I will find the reward for my courage and my virtues."[58] She went further and offered a defence of the Girondins. "They had talent, virtues, character; those were their crimes. They are the sages of the Republic!"[59]

When the contents of her writings are considered, it is a wonder that she lasted as long as she did. Her trespasses against those in power had been many. From the time of her critique of Robespierre she knew that her days were numbered. In the dedication of her works to Philippe Egalité in the autumn of 1793 she wrote, "My days are threatened; I address myself to you in order to protect them and you know that I do not fear death, but I wish to die gloriously and if I am able, I will still serve my country in my last moments."[60]

However, it had been the posting of *Les Trois Urnes, ou la salut de la patrie, par un voyageur aérien* in July of 1793 that had supplied the final provocation. The idea behind it was freedom of choice. The people should choose the form that the government should take by means of a secret ballot tossed into an urn labelled according to type; republican, federal, or monarchical. In this way the French people would be masters of their fate. They would be able to choose the government which best suited their needs, conforming best to character, mores, climate. At the time of the posting of this piece, de

Olympe de Gouges. (Medallion)

Gouges was making preparations to move to Tours but was in still in Paris. Upon completing her poster, *Les Trois Urnes,* she made arrangements to have her message distributed around the city. She was arrested on the Rue Barillerie close to the Palais de Justice as she returned home on the morning of 20 July. She was taken to the Mairie and held there for five days. On the morning of July 25 she was moved to the Abbaye prison where she stayed until August 21 at which time she was transferred to the Petite-Force; on October 15 she went to the convalescent home of one Dr. Lescourbiac. From there she was moved on October 20 to the Conciergerie, already known as the "anti-chamber of death." Throughout this period of imprisonment she continued to write and as always left a detailed account of her thoughts and experiences.

In August she wrote *Défense d'Olympe de Gouges face au Tribunal Révolutionnaire.* In it she lamented the suffering she had endured since her arrest and complained of the violation of the Constitution, emphasizing that liberty of opinion and of the press was a sacred right. She queried whether these rights were merely vague and illusory. She complained that she had been found guilty without a trial and was a victim of a "conspiracy of blood." She stated that Robespierre was trying to pass her off as being insane. She retorted that sane or reasonable, the welfare of her country was her first concern, and predicted that the whole country would disintegrate if true Republicans failed to rally around the statue of liberty.[61] The miseries of her incarceration she recounted in detail, lamenting that the public would find it difficult to believe the conditions under which she was forced to live, particularly the total lack of privacy and the inattention to medical necessities.[62]

The writings of this period demonstrate that de Gouges realized that her chances of survival were slim indeed. On 22 September she wrote a letter fron the Petite-Force which she addressed to Forty-Eight Sections. In it she donated her collected writings to the citizens of Paris, saying, "Citizens...you know my love for my country and for liberty. Accept the entire edition of my works...and send a deputation to the bar of the senate in order to reinstate justice and the maintenance of laws."[63] One of the police inspectors, Latour-Lamontagne, commented in his report on 21 September as follows:

> All the walls of Paris arc covered by a poster of the Citizenness Olympe de Gouges who complains of her long detention, recalls the services which she has rendered to the *Patrie;* and announces the preparation of a new massacre in the prisons and regards herself as a victim that is going to be immolated. The poster produces no reaction; [passersby] pause for a moment and then move on, saying, 'Oh! It's Olympe de Gouges.'[64]

Throughout the time of her imprisonment de Gouges was also soliciting freedom in letters she wrote to various persons in authority, such as Danton and Fouquier-Tinville. The response was minimal. She was interrogated on 6 August while at the Abbaye prison by members of the Revolutionary Tribunal who were interested mainly in the content of *Les Trois Urnes* and what they interpreted to be a call for a type of government other than the "Republic one and indivisible."[65] De Gouges was returned to her cell to await her fate. Finally, after three more months of imprisonment, with the Terror at its height, she was called before the Revolutionary Tribunal on 2 November, 1793. She was to follow in the footsteps of the queen, Marie-Antoinette, and twenty-one Girondins who had been executed in October. De Gouges was taken from her cell in the Conciergerie at about seven a.m. and led to the "Room of Equality" where her trial commenced, under the direction of Naulin, substitute for the public prosecutor, Fouquier-Tinville. The charges against her were read and proved to be lengthy in number and duration. She was accused, among other things, of attempting to restore the tyrant that the people itself had seen fit to depose, of having claimed in one of her works that the monarchy was the best form of government for the "spirit of France," and of provoking civil war. Further, it was charged that she had attempted to undermine the constituted authorities, slander the friends and defenders of the people and of liberty, and cause trouble between the people and their representatives.[66] To her surprise she was left with no one to defend her and she was told that she was capable of carrying out her own defence. As the trial proceeded it became evident that it was turning on the content of *Les Trois Urnes*, the authorities being particularly offended by the phrase "Louis Capet is dead, but he reigns still among you." This phrase expressed the idea that the French people had "the Republic on their lips, but royalism in their hearts." The suggestion that there should be a choice between three types of government was interpreted as being particularly threatening. However, de Gouges steadfastly insisted throughout her trial that all her concern and all her efforts had been for the good of her country. In the end she announced in one last desperate and melodramatic act, that her enemies would not have the pleasure of seeing her blood flow because she was pregnant. This astounding announcement apparently caused a great deal of laughter from the spectators.

These events were recorded tersely in *Le Moniteur* under the heading *Tribunal Criminel Révolutionnaire,* wherein the readership was informed almost daily of death sentences handed out to citizens for various acts of disloyalty to the *Nation.*

> Olympe de Gouges, the widow Aubrey, writer, age thirty-eight, native of
> Montauban, convicted of being the author of writings advocating the establish-
> ment of a power which challenges the sovereignty of the people, has been con-
> demned to death. She has declared herself pregnant. The execution has been
> deferred until she has been examined by the appropriate people. [67]

On 6 November, *Le Moniteur* reported that the examination of de Gouges had demonstrated her declaration of pregnancy to be false and therefore "the delay had been lifted and the execution had taken place the 13 Brumaire (3 November).[68]

Le Moniteur had published on 17 November the following extract from *La Feuille de Salut Public:*

> Olympe de Gouges, born with an exalted imagination, took her deliriousness for
> an inspiration of nature. She began with being unreasonable and ended by adopt-
> ing the goal of the evil people who wished to divide France; she wished to be a
> statesman and it appears that the law should punish this conspirator for having
> forgotten the virtues appropriate to her sex.[69]

Far from being the veritable "amazon of the pen"[70] that was Olympe de Gouges, Théroigne de Méricourt participated in the Revolution as an agitator and street activist. Her career was a checkered one until the time that she became enchanted with revolutionary ideas and beliefs. She is said, perhaps somewhat more romantically than scientifically, to have died of a malady known as "revolutionary fever," but before the onset of the illness that eventually caused her death, she led an active and involved existence. Born Anne-Josephe Terwagne in 1762 in Marcourt-sur-Ourthe in the province of Luxembourg, about forty miles from Liège, she left home at an early age, worked at a variety of menial jobs, and eventually decided to become a singer. She lived in London, Geneva, and Rome as well as in Paris.[71]

She has been surrounded by myth. Known as "la belle Liègeoise," she captured the hearts and imaginations of many people, including the historians of the nineteenth century. She was often portrayed as the sword-wielding woman in a riding cloak, sometimes mounted on a white horse, who directed the action in the streets during some of the most memorable days of the Revolution. She has been called "chameleon", "passionate lover," and "vindictive and bloody amazon."[72] Although the written record of her participation is not extensive, her *Confessions, Memoires,* and letters do supply some details of her involvement with the Revolution.

Rumour said that she had played a major role in the storming of the Bastille in July, 1789 and witnesses at the Châtelet inquiry claimed to have seen her on the march during the October Days of that same year. It was said that she was responsible for the murder of a royalist journalist, Suleau, on 10 August, 1792. Much of the fascination with de Méricourt comes from the fact that she was a shadowy participant in the *grandes journées* of the Revolution and her actual role has remained shrouded in myth. Her own *Confessions* clarify to a certain extent many third person accounts that have contributed to the legendary persona. She explains the change in her name, saying that she dropped Anne-Josephe and became Théroigne, a derivative of the family name. She stated, "I am called Théroigne, a derivative of my family name and I was born at Marcour. It is at Paris and at Versailles where I was given my surname which is only a form of the name Marcour."[73]

De Méricourt also described her uncertain position during the spring

of 1789 which proved instrumental to her return to Paris and ultimately in her entry into the revolutionary arena. She was in Geneva
in April and of that period in her life she said, "I did not know where
to go. Should it be Rome, London, Luxembourg? Should it be France
where my interests demanded my presence .... I was perplexed."[74]
She was captivated by the issues being discussed in France and when
she heard about the formation of a National Assembly open to all she
declared her enthusiasm. She made her decisions and left Geneva on
30 April, heading back to France in order to straighten out her business affairs and "to be a witness to such a great spectacle."[75]

She took up residence in the Hôtel de Toulouse in Paris and later
admitted that at first she really had very little understanding of the
Revolution. "I occupied myself with music and read the daily journals, which I understood hardly at all." But the general atmosphere
of excitement influenced her thoughts and activities and even though
she admitted to having no notion of the unrecognized rights of the
people, she proclaimed that she had nonetheless a love of liberty.
She began to attend the meetings of the National Assembly on a regular basis. She later stated that "an instinct which I cannot define
made me approve of the Revolution, without really knowing why,
because I had no instruction. The little that I know I have learned
little by little through observing the meetings of the National Assembly."[76]

One persistent myth deals with her participation on 14 July, 1789.
It placed her in the street at the first sign of an uprising. She was
described as having played a leading role, being everywhere at once,
giving orders and having them obeyed. She was, supposedly, with
the leaders at the Bastille, placing detachments at the barricades in

the principal locations, stopping the dispatches that were coming from the court at Versailles to Paris, and finally, she organized the "undisciplined and newly armed" masses.[77] According to de Méricourt, the facts were somewhat different. She maintained that on the evening of 12 July, the day after the Revolution exploded, she was walking in the streets with a maid. She described her naiveté, saying that when she encountered soldiers she asked them if they were for the Third Estate. She was chased down the street for her efforts until the soldiers realized that she was simply an "isolated" and "curious" woman.[78] She maintained that she was never at the Bastille but had been instead at the Palais Royale when the news arrived that the Bastille had been successfully taken. It appears that she was telling the truth because the only woman whose name was recorded among the conquerors of the Bastille was Marie Charpentier.

Despite all this, the myths surrounding de Méricourt continued to grow. Whether the poets of the nineteenth century made the legend or whether they merely recorded it is uncertain, but we do know that they used the theme of *la belle Liègeoise,* who was not from Liège but from Marcourt, for their poetry. Barthélemy, Mathieu, and Baudelaire praised her as heroine of the great days of the Revolution.[79] The image began with the Bastille and was magnified after the events of the October Days and her supposed participation there. She explains in her confessions that she moved to Versailles during the summer of 1789 because she was fascinated with the events in the National Assembly and wished to be in a place where she could readily observe what was going on. Her interest had been piqued by her walks around the Palais Royale. There she witnessed enormous changes taking place in the attitudes of the people who frequented the area, observing, she said "the aura of a new time." She was struck by the air of general goodwill that prevailed. "Egoïsme seemed to have been banished from all hearts. There was no more class distinction." She went so far as to say that people even looked different, that each person now dared to "publicly develop his character and natural faculties." Many people, she said, possessed "a heroic air" and it was generally impossible for a person of intelligence to ignore such a spectacle. De Méricourt explained that she gave in to the "irresistible enthusiasm"which engulfed her and she resolved to go to Versailles in order to observe the sessions of the National Assembly.

She went to live on the Rue de Noailles in Versailles and at the time when she arrived there the Assembly had just begun to debate the *Declaration of the Rights of Man and Citizen* . She found that the Assembly offered "a beautiful and noble spectacle" and she was struck by the majesty of it. At first, she confessed, her understanding of the proceedings was extremely limited, but gradually she began to see the plight of the people as opposed to the situation of the privileged in French society. She explained that her sympathy for the people grew with her understanding and that it transformed itself into an "ardent love" when she became persuaded that justice and right were on the side of the people.[80]

The details of de Méricourt's association with the events of the October Days are sketchy. At the Châtelet inquiry several witnesses reported that they saw her in the streets of Versailles during the late afternoon and evening of the fifth and on the morning of the sixth. It was reported that she had been seen in a red riding cape, sometimes on horseback, among the troops of the Flanders regiment.[81] She denied having played an active role, saying that she barely remembered what day the king came to Paris. She said she wore "Amazon white" and a round cap and that she spoke to no one.[82] She testified that she was in the Assembly on the evening of the fifth, but left before the proceedings adjourned. She then stayed in the streets merely as a witness.

On the morning of 6 October she reported that she left her dwelling at about six a.m. to find the Assembly just open, the National Guard in front of the chateau, and a huge crowd gathered there. She observed many things, she was to testify, but participated virtually not at all. She denied ever having been mounted on a horse or having in any way disturbed the Flanders regiment, which, she said, had been "calm, in good order, and in battle formation."[83] In this way de Méricourt denied the involvement widely attributed to her in these events.

After the October Days she moved back to Paris, stating that she followed the National Assembly there. She continued to observe the sessions, morning and evening. She declared that everyone there knew her, due both to her patriotism and her irreproachable conduct in her private life. She recounted in her *Confessions* how her idea of giving civic crowns and cockades to patriots in the National Assembly was popular and successful. She was mercilessly lampooned in the royalist press for an incident which occurred 14 February, 1790. She had accompanied the procession of deputies of the National Assembly during the *Te Deum* at Notre dame. In her *Confessions* she explained the situation saying that she had arrived too late and could not get through the crowd. Several of the deputies invited her to join the procession and she accepted the offer. She said that others who

Théroigne de Méricourt. Courtesy Musée Carnavalet.

were not deputies were also there but they were all men. Of her persecution around this incident, she stated, that she was extremely humiliated and that she once again observed "the force and existence of pride and masculine prejudice which oppresses my sex and maintains it in servitude."[84]

In February, 1790, de Méricourt was kidnapped by two French émigrés, hired by the royalist Mercy-Argenteau, while she was staying in a small village in Luxembourg. She was accused of having plotted to kill Marie-Antoinette and was taken on a gruelling journey which terminated in the Austrian prison of Kufstein. There she was imprisoned until the following November and in her *Confessions* she described the mental and physical anguish of this period. The charges against her were never proven and she was articulate and intelligent in her defence. Mercy-Argenteau's actual motive was the hope that he or his agents would be able to obtain valuable information from her about what was happening in France. He thought that she would have much information about people and events there, about revolutionary agents in the Low Countries, and about the intended fate of the royal family. Their victim had nothing to tell them and did not hesitate to express her opinion that the whole affair was a gross miscarriage of justice. She described her persecutors as abominable and hideous liars, saying "not only is their goal to incriminate and defile an innocent woman, but they tend also to compromise and dishonour persons who are respectable and deserving of the esteem of the public." She raged that there did not exist an inhabitant of Paris who would not declare, in hearing of her ordeal, that such "absurdity and ineptitude" could not be surpassed.[85]

When released in November she went first to Vienna and then to

Brussels. She was told by officials that she must not return to France but she chose to ignore this restriction and by January she was back in Paris, telling her story and being regarded as a patriot and heroine by her many admirers. She enjoyed a memorable reception at the Jacobin Club on 26 January, 1792 accompanied by an invitation to write an account of her persecutions and present it at the next meeting.[86]   At the beginning of February she presented the club with a detailed account of her incarceration to which the membership reacted with "lively indignation' and she received great praise for her loyalty and constancy. It was reported the de Méricourt advocated war as a means of dealing with enemies and she stated that the Revolution had supporters "in the Low Countries, in Germany, and even in the palace of the emperor."[87]   From this time forward she was regarded as a follower of Brissot in other words, a Girondin. The introduction of her February presentation indicates that she was at this time at the height of her influence and popularity. Introduced by the head of the Commune, she was described as "one of the first amazons of liberty," "martyr of the Constitution," and "president of her sex."[88]

On 25 March, 1792 de Méricourt delivered her famous address to the *Société Fraternelle des Minimes* in which she advocated the formation of battalions of females to serve in the defence of the nation. "We will arm ourselves because it is reasonable that we prepare ourselves to defend our rights [and] our homes." Women should not be prevented by the "faintheartedness contracted during our slavery," from coming forward in defence of the *patrie.*[89]   She went on to say that the example of women's devotion would awaken in the souls of men an overwhelming passion of love of glory and of the *patrie* and she alluded to the strength of women in the past.

> Women! the same blood ran always in our veins; what we did at Beauvais, at Versailles, the 5 and 6 October, and in many other important and decisive circumstances, proves that we are not strangers to magnanimous sentiments.[90]

On 23 April de Méricourt interrupted a meeting of the Jacobin Club as a result of remarks made by Collot d'Herbois, one of the members. He reported that she had stated in the Café Hottot on the Terrasse de Feuillants that she had withdrawn her support from him and from Robespierre. According to the club minutes, there was general laughter in response to his statement. De Méricourt's response was immediate and energetic. She jumped over the barrier and approached the Chair despite efforts to restrain her. She tried to insist upon speaking but she was escorted outside and the President declared the meeting ended.

Problems confronting the Revolution in the spring of 1792 were many. In April France declared war on Austria. The Girondin ministry, formed in March, was dissolved in June. On the twentieth of June, a date which marked the double anniversary of the Tennis Court Oath (1789) and the flight of the king to Varennes (1791), an insurrection took place in Paris. Exactly what role Théroigne de Méricourt played that day is uncertain. Legend has it that the young and beautiful woman, "dressed as a man,, a sword in her hand, a gun on her shoulder, and sitting on a cannon" was de Méricourt.[91] It was even claimed that she pushed the wheel of the cannon that was hoisted to the second floor of the Tuileries Palace.[92] In reality, evidence, or lack of it, points to her absence from the events of that day. There is no sure evidence that she was part of one of the processions that went from the Faubourgs St. Antoine and St. Marcel to the Tuileries or even that she was part of the crowd that assembled there. There is evidence, however, that she was active the day before. A police report of 20 June deals with the plots against the king of which the people of the two faubourgs are suspected. It deals as well with the "provocations" addressed to the people by de Méricourt in support of these plans on 19 June. No serious documentation has been found to date to say that she was an active participant in the events that took place during the day on 20 June.

It seems, rather, that it was on 10 August that de Méricourt did appear in the role of revolutionary heroine, where royalist tradition had placed her during the October Days. If not exactly a heroine, at least she is known to have played an active leadership role in the events of 10 August and was later recognized by the Paris Commune for her efforts. She is said to have incensed the crowds with inflammatory speeches and her name is linked with that of François-Louis Suleau because of her participation in the bloody activities of that day. Suleau was a collaborator on the royalist journal *Actes des Apôtres* which had often pilloried Théroigne de Méricourt.[93] On the morning of 10 August Suleau was arrested on the Terrasse des Feuillants. He was wearing the uniform of a grenadier of the National Guard and was carrying false papers. He was taken to the Tuileries Section and held with several other known royalists who had been incarcerated during he night. As the crowd gathered at the Tuileries, these men became the target of increasing popular fury. Some managed to flee but nine were unable to escape, of which Suleau was one. The crowd wished to execute these captives and became increasingly insistent. When de Méricourt made her appearance the

crowd was already out of hand. According to some accounts, she did
not even recognize Suleau until a woman in the crowd called his
name.[94] It was reported that while the crowd was howling for blood,
de Méricourt, brandishing a sword, arrived and claimed the prisoners in the name of the people. The president of the section, Bonjour,
had only about two hundred soldiers and he did not in any way resist
the wishes of the crowd. Suleau's murder took place in the midst of
the howling crowd and afterwards, it was reported, de Méricourt
jumped into the middle of the Marseillais troops who in turn knocked
over the fence surrounding the Carousel. She was reportedly in-
jured.[95] On 3 September the *Moniteur* reported that the Marseillais
troops had just bestowed civic crowns on Claire Lacombe, Théroigne
de Méricourt, and Reine Audu "who had distinguished themselves
by their courage on the day of 10 August."[96]

No proof exists that Suleau's murder was actually committed by
de Méricourt, but she is generally regarded as being "more or less"
responsible for the bloody event. All accounts do agree that she was,
on 10 August, in a state of aggravated revolutionary fervour and was
an enthusiastic participant in the activities of the crowd. An account
in the *Moniteur*, generally assumed to be a description of her, illustrates the extent of her emotion and involvement. The eye-witness
stated that he had seen a young woman, sword in hand, standing on a
rock. He claimed that he had heard her harangue the crowd. She
declared the *patrie* endangered. Saving the country, she told her
audience, depended upon their arms, their courage, and their patriotism. "Arm yourselves, therefore, and hasten to the Tuileries Palace.
It is there that you will find your principal enemies." She exhorted
the crowd to exterminate this "race of vipers" which had for three

years conspired against the people. She warned that in eight days the people would be exterminated if they did not achieve victory this day and she proclaimed that the crowd must choose between life and death, between liberty and slavery. According to the same witness there were many women active in the crowd that day, some armed with swords, others armed with pikes. He claimed to have seen some women kill the Swiss bodyguards and others were busy encouraging their husbands, children, brothers. Some of the women were killed,he said, but it did not intimidate the others whom he heard shouting, "Let the Prussians come, and the Austrians as well; we may lose everyone, but not one of these assholes is going to survive."[97]

De Méricourt was quiet during the months that followed. There is no evidence that she played any part in the September Massacres and little historical record of her activities. During this period France faced increasing problems and the conflict within the Convention between the Jacobins and the Girondins accelerated. Her fortune was now depleted and she lived in a room on the Rue St.-Honoré, close to the Jacobin Club and the Salle du Manège. She remained a supporter of the Girondins and her *Address to the Forty-Eight Sections,* written approximately 10 May, 1793, strongly reflected some of their views. In it she warned against the foreigners on French soil whose goal it was to incite civil war. She also expressed the opinion that because of political differences at home, the loyalties of the French troops were divided and confused. She proposed a system whereby women would participate in patriotic life in a positive but non-military manner, unlike the proposals made in 1792 for battalions of female soldiers. The task of the women would be to improve virtue and patriotism among the people and to supply a general atmosphere of support and encouragement for soldiers. "Their reward would be to have a distinguished place in our national celebrations and to supervise schools dedicated to our sex."[98]

On 15 May de Méricourt was to become involved in an altercation with women belonging to the *Club des Citoyennes Républicaines Révolutionnaires,* an event that would signal the end of her public life. The women of the club were Jacobin supporters and were becoming more and more strident and violent in the expression of their opinions. On the morning of 15 May, de Méricourt encountered a group of these women on the Terrasse des Feuillants as she went as usual to observe the Convention. Reports say that she angered them by making remarks in favor of Brissot, a Girondin leader. She was stripped by the angry women who then subjected her to a public whipping. Police reports of the incident stated that the women believed her to be a traitor or "false patriot" and that she had said that she would make them "bite the dust" sooner or later.[99] On 18 May the *Révolutions de Paris* described the incident, saying,

> ...for several days a number of women policed the Tuileries garden and the corridors of the National Convention, undertaking to check for cockades and to arrest people who looked suspicious to them. It was these women who, on Wednesday the fifteenth, whipped Théroigne while calling her a Brissotine.[100]

From this time on, sources record only the rapid decline of her mental stability, her increasing confusion, and details of her hospitalization. A substantial amount has been written on this phase of her life. She sank rapidly into dementia and on 24 September 1794 she was officially declared insane by a health official in the Pelletier section. At this time she was already resident in a house of detention in that district. She was released later in the year and then hospitalized early in the new year. From this time on it was a matter of being shuffled from one mental institution to the next. She was incarcerated in the Maison des Folles de la Salpêtrière for the last ten years of her life.

This woman is often regarded as having embodied, in both myth and reality, the very spirit of the Revolution. "Surrounded by a legend woven in blood, madness, and hysteria,"[101] she participated with dedication and enthusiasm in the remarkable events of many of the great days. One unflattering contemporary portrait likened the pattern of her life and political involvement to that of the Revolution itself.

> At the end of her career she had absolutely lost all her graces. She was pale, vitriolic, emaciated. Finally, she was the living embodiment of the Revolution. Brilliant in its beginnings, fanatical during its course, disgusting in filth and blood after 10 August.[102]

No doubt the reality of the situation was somewhat less melodramatic. Théroigne de Méricourt was most likely the unfortunate victim of some illness which resulted in the slow disintegration of her mental faculties and which led eventually to her death in June of 1817 at the age of fifty-five.

Each of these women, the "amazon of the pen" no less that the "amazon of the sword," made her own contribution to the Revolution. Each deserves recognition for her participation and dedication and each historical profile is to some extent representative of the broader female involvement.

THE SECOND SEX IN THE SECOND CITY

Of the few women's clubs for which detailed information exists, one was located in France's second city, Lyon, which had a particularly active women's organization established quite early in the Revolution and for which some interesting accounts are available. It evolved from the fraternal *Société du Concert* which was established in February, 1791 and which held its meetings, open to the public, at the *Pères de l'Oratoire.* It had a membership of approximately two thousand people. Women were admitted and as a sign of patriotism they had to wear a tricolour ribbon.[103] It seems that many women attended the meetings and it was not long before they attempted to organize their own club. In June, 1791 women went as a group to participate in prayers for two prisoners executed for debt and formed a procession to the cathedral to hear the mass and *Te Deum.*[104] In August the women appointed a provisional president, the citizeness Sobry, who must have suffered a loss of self-confidence almost immediately in that she called on her husband to take that position and she became vice-president. Nonetheless, this was still considered to be a women's club, despite the fact that a male now presided. The charter demanded that members wear a medallion at public ceremonies and that they take the following oath:

> I swear to be faithful to the nation, to the law, and to the king. I swear to support at every opportunity my husband, my brothers, and my children to fulfil their duties toward the Nation. I swear to teach my children and all others over which I have authority to prefer death to slavery.[105]

The meetings were held every Sunday at the hour of Vespers in a house on the Rue du Pas-Etroit at the corner of the Rue Commarmont. On Sundays and holidays the society marched in a procession displaying the flag of Saint-Jean.[106] The *Révolutions de Paris* took unfavorable notice of the new women's club at Lyon.

> In the name of the Nation, in the name of Nature, in the name of good morals of which the women's clubs are the plagues, because of the dissipation that they [the women] cause with them, let them stay at home and watch over their households.[107]

In Lyon as well the club was a victim of unkind criticism. In a *Déclaration burlesque des droits de la femme* published there shortly after the club had its first meeting, Articles I and XVII satirically proclaimed the following:

> Women are born, live, and die with the right to talk. They are equal in this respect. Distinctions between them can only be founded on the more or less grand perfection of the organs of speech.... The art of being unreasonable is for women an inherent right and cannot be taken away; no female can be deprived of it up until such time that it pleases Nature to make them differently.[108]

In January, 1792, the group, now called the *Citoyennes de Lyon Composant l'Association Séante aux Jacobins de Lyon,* presented their charter to the *Société des Jacobins* in Paris and requested affiliation with them. Despite the fact that the women were sincere and dedicated in their club activities it appears that they were never really taken seriously. Their invitations and addresses to the municipal and governmental committees were largely ignored.[109] The *Journal de Lyon* of 9 January, 1793 gave the minutes of a club meeting which had been held on 30 December, 1792. The editor of the journal introduced the topic with words of support and encouragement. He said that while many popular societies had abandoned all useful activities, the women's club of Lyon had prepared itself by means of instructive gatherings for the responsibilites that the nation was now imposing upon them. This "society of mothers" who study the forms of the new government inspire in their children "love of their country, respect for its laws, the conservation of their rights, and the faithful observation of their duties." These women had certainly earned, in the opinion of the editor at least, a right to respect.[110] The editor encouraged the women to keep up their interesting work, saying that they had been entrusted with the responsibility of preparing the future generation for the difficult demands of liberty. Noting that all his generation had been raised to servile habits under the monarchy, he added that his generation was now ready to fight in defence of liberty and that it was the children who were now about to reap the rewards of the work of the parents. They would learn from the mistakes of their elders. "Mothers, give us men, form citizens, and you will be a credit to your country."

The article reported that the meeting began as usual with the reading of the minutes of the last one. Then a member asked for the singing of the Marseillaise and two young members obliged, accompanied by music and the whole membership in chorus. At this time delegates arrived representing department, district, and city governments respectively. These individuals took their places beside the president. This group was immediately questioned by President Charton and Citoyenne Charpine. The president spoke to them about their responsibilities to their countrymen and Citoyenne Charpine emphasized the necessity of formulating a new catechism so that children would come to understand the grandeur of the Supreme Being and "the principles of a true republican." Next Citizeness Peyre mounted the tribune and in her address stated that "we owe our glorious Revolution to the *philosophes* that came before us." She em-

phasized the importance of propagating the popular societies so that
the young people could be instructed in the new laws. Then the
Citizeness Machezot delivered to the visitors a speech in which she
promised them in the name of the Assembly the greatest reward of
true republicans for their endeavours, that being "the glory of truly
being a credit to their country."

It is obvious that all these addresses were strongly patriotic in theme,
as was the speech of one of the younger members of the society. A
young girl mounted the tribune and recited Chapter Seven and part
of Chapter Eight of Rousseau's *Social Contract.* She also recited the
Declaration of the Rights of Man and Citizen along with a patriotic
prayer. More of the same followed with other young members taking part. Prizes were awarded to the participants and some of these,
interestingly enough, were boys. The first prizes were presented by
the representatives of the department, the second by the representatives of the district, and the third by those of the municipality. One
of the young boys took an oath not to use the sabre with which he
had been decorated for any purpose other than "to overthrow the
enemies of the *patrie* and the Republic."

The meeting continued with speeches from the government representatives. Citizen Maillard, representing the Department, reviewed
the responsibilities that each citizen must take in order to consolidate
the new republic. He emphasized the responsibilities that these
"citizeness mothers of families" had to their children. Citizen
Marezon, who was representing the district, took as his theme, the
importance of the mothers' role in instructing their children. Citizen
Bertholon, spoke of the importance of spreading the society's principles of patriotism and of the responsibilities of mothers in bringing

happiness to their fellow citizens. Women must not forget, of course, that even while participating enthusiastically in the birth of the new nation and its institutions, somebody still had to attend to domestic duties. Who better to jog their memories on this point than the male representatives of the new governing bodies? The editor of the *Journal de Lyon* added the following note:

> We have resisted the temptation to give the minutes in full. Pure principles, wise patriotism, truly Republican simplicity, this is the example which the citizenesses of Lyon give to all the friends of equality....We must add that by a decree of the society, analogous to the one of the General Council of the Commune, a collection of more than one thousand *livres* destined for the purchase of pikes, has been distributed to women whose husbands are at the front.[111]

Extracts of the minutes of the next meeting appeared in the same journal on January 10, 1793. Once again the women mounted the tribune to make patriotic speeches. Citizeness Peyre pointed out that "the time has come when the glamour of error will soon disappear and the veil of lies is torn away. Truth triumphs and shines with its natural simplicity." The perfect society, she thought, was at hand. Tyrants were falling. Soon all classes would march together under the flag of liberty and equality. She stressed the responsibility of the Society in matters of public education. It was necessary, she stated, to give to children a catechism from which they would learn the "grandeur of the Supreme Being," without forgetting that they are also citizens. The same catechism should teach them what it is that they owe to God and what it is that they owe to their country. Another speaker admonished citizenesses to do their part at home while the men were at the front defending them. This speaker emphasized that they were entrusted with maintaining tranquillity and should guard against being influenced by malevolent people."[112]

The editors of *Révolutions de Paris* had other opinions. In its issue of the week of 19 January it dealt harshly once again with the club at Lyon. The article began with a description of an ideal political involvement for women, stating that there could be nothing more uplifting or more useful than a group of good mothers from the same neighbourhood meeting each day at a designated time, children on their laps, and work in hand. They would consult each other on the duties of their station. Their husbands would return each evening to share with them the events of the day and, of course, play the role of superior intellect and political educator by reading to their wives the daily decrees of the National Assembly. That being completely natural, there would be nothing to say about it. But what about this women's club that has just opened at Lyon? That, surely, was quite a different matter. Although the editors would assuredly be the first to pay homage to the purity of the intentions of these good women, they questioned why the women held to such a strict agenda for their meetings and why they took minutes. Why invite the three administrative bodies to observe the meetings? And why did President Charton and the Citoyenne Charpine address the magistrates in order to ask for a new catechism which would be "more to the order of the day?" What was the problem with the old one? Why, queried the editor, would a mother need such a thing as a book from which to instruct her children?

> Has she not a book of nature and of her heart? Is the father not the first teacher? What could the young girls learn from Rousseau's *Contrat social* that they could not have learned from Lafontaine's fairy tales?[113]

The good women of Lyon should stay home "in the name of the

nation," "in the name of nature," and "in the name of good domestic principles." The editors reasoned that due to the dissipation that the clubs caused among women, the women of Lyons should stay at home and "watch over their households without asking the Bishop Lamourette for reform of the catechism."[114] Others shared that opinion. The president of the *Club Central de Lyon* expressed in an address to members his open distrust, probably hatred, of women in general. It was reported in *Le Journal de la Société Populaire des amis de la consitution établie à Lyon* that President Grandchamp proclaimed that among the many types of enemies the most formidable are those who get hold of man in the cradle and set him on the wrong path "until decrepitude." He explained in more detail that "These enemies inhabit our homes, touch us, are dear to us, and we are their slaves." Who were they? They were the "more beautiful half of the human race and not the more happy, this frivolous sex which is the happiness and the torment of the other." This was the enemy who "takes revenge for her natural weakness by capturing strength by deceit; who hides under flowers chains of bronze." These enemies "render servile the wisest men." Women, he proclaimed, held absolute sway over opinion. He believed that women should not be shocked by his straightforward expression of the truth and therefore he felt that he could continue. He said that women are enclosed all their lives in a circle of a small number of frivolous acquaintances and therefore are the first victims of ignorance. "Weak, sensitive, delicate, such is their nature. Such is also the route by which fanaticism, prejudice, obstinancy take over their souls." These weaknesses had a direct bearing on the Revolution, according to President Grandchamp, who declared that "These are the principal sources

of evils which have disfigured the Revolution more than once."[115]
It is obvious from the words of the worthy President Grandchamp
that not all Lyonnais were in favor of the women's club. Vehement
opposition did exist.

The women of Lyon truly came into their own during the difficult
days of the autumn of 1792 when fear of an invasion by foreign armies resulted in panic and widespread disorder from which their city
was not immune. The women, fearing widespread hoarding and starvation, rioted in the streets for three days in mid-September. From
September sixteenth to eighteenth they became "female police
commissioners" and they took over the markets and boutiques. They
posted a notice to the residents of the city which announced that the
sovereign people of Lyon, having lived for years under the tyranny
of the "'aristocratic monopolists," had suffered enough. They were
exhausted from enduring four years in which the value of paper money
which they had received for their work and their sweat had steadily
declined. They were also exhausted from paying ever-increasing
prices for the basic necessities of life and they had now decreed that
they would pay the prices for daily necessities only as set forth on
this list. Sixty items were listed which would be subject to price
control. The poster explained that abiding by this decree would demonstrate a patriotism which worked truly for the good of the people.
It would result in a just distribution between that which was earned
and that which was spent on a daily basis. Those citizens who con-
formed to "the will of the people," in other words those who adhered
to the decree, "which is founded only on the basis of justice, equity,
and equality," would be respected by their fellow citizens and would
find in them "guardians of their faith and of their property." On the

other hand, those who did not listen or who dared to oppose the will of the people in some manner would be publicly disgraced and generally regarded as traitors to the nation. They would be ordered to conform to the decree and to sell their merchandise for the same price that they had paid for it.[116]

The role of the women in the dramatic events which took place in Lyon during 1793 is not well documented. The Girondins took over the city in late May with help from resident sympathizers. Montagnard forces laid siege to the city until it fell in early October. It is difficult, if not impossible, to find, in even the most recent analysis of this period, much information on the activities or fate of the women's clubs in these events,[117] but fragments of interesting information on the *Lyonnaises* are available. When the Revolutionary Army entered Lyon in late November, its commander, Ronsin, noted that most men remained in hiding, and only a few women stood along the way. In their faces, he said, could be read "more indignation than fear." A few days later, a petition purportedly signed by 10,000 women of Lyon appealed to Collot d'Herbois and Fouché, the representatives on mission there, for mercy for the thousands of men incarcerated. The appeal was sternly rejected and Collot on his return to Paris severely criticized the people of Lyon, in particular the women, who, he reported to the Jacobin Club, were "plunged madly into adultery and prostitution."[118]

Liberty (always depicted as a female form). Courtesy Musée Carnavalet.

CHAPTER THREE

LA SOCIETE DES CITOYENNES REPUBLICAINES REVOLUTIONNAIRES

Elles peuvent éclairer leurs epoux, leur communiquer des réflexions précieuses, fruit du calme d'une vie sédentaire. (They [women] are able to enlighten their husbands, communicate to them their precious reflections, the result of the tranquillity of a sedentary life.) Deputy Amar of the Isère in the National Convention, October 30, 1793.

ORIGINS

The formation of the *Société des Citoyennes Républicaines Révolutionnaires* took place over several months in the spring of 1793. The threat of foreign war which occurred after the Declaration of Pillnitz in August, 1791 brought all club activity to a more intensely political orientation than it had previously enjoyed. During the winter and spring of 1792 the women in the clubs redirected their activities, turning from *fêtes,* education, and philanthropy to matters of political interest. By February of 1793 the women of Paris openly expressed the desire for an organization independent of male dominance.

In February a group of women who were later to form the membership of the *Citoyennes* approached the Jacobin society with a request for a place to meet.[1] They were not enthusiastically received and the president announced that "a deputation of women from the section of Quatre Nations requests the use of the meeting room of the Jacobins for next day at four o'clock." The purpose would be a discussion on hoarding. One of the Jacobin members, François Desfieux, responded that the room was occupied every afternoon by members of another club, the *Société des Défenseurs de la République Une et Indivisible des 83 Départements.* The women would only be able to occupy the room in the morning. They could, however, use the meeting room of the *Société fraternelle,* which contained eight hundred seats, in the afternoon. At this time Robespierre stated his objections to the whole idea, saying that "too many discussions on food are alarming to the Republic." With that the members tried to go ahead with the daily business. However, the crowd in the galleries refused to be silenced and there were shouts that merchants and carpetbaggers were present who "enrich themselves from public misfortune." Calm could not be restored and the president tried to explain that the members did not have jurisdiction over the disposal of the meeting room during the day. One of the members, obviously a theorist, spoke on the necessity of conquering freedom first and food at a reasonable price would certainly follow. He said that as president of the Convention he had "repulsed with horror" a petition whose object was a tax on food. In response the tumult began again. A member stated that if permission were granted for a meeting of women, then thirty thousand women would incite disorder in Paris. Another member responded that a remedy would be to rid the popular societies of the individuals who bring up this topic for purposes of inciting disorder. He went on to say that this was not the moment to act, that the question of *denrées* (basic necessities) was not on the agenda and that such discussion would serve to compromise the calm and tranquillity which he saw as being so necessary to their situation. "The Society," he said, "must occupy itself, unperturbed, with the examination of the Constitution, and no other matter is to be put on the agenda before that one is settled."[2] This emotional exchange leaves little doubt that the Jacobins feared the increasing participation of women in matters of politics and that they were determined to squelch any possibility of a female insurrection before it began.

This question of subsistences brought before the Jacobins at this time had occupied women in their roles as wives and mothers for a very long time. How were they to obtain enough food to sustain their families in times of severe shortages? The intermingling of the economic considerations and political objectives provides a constant in the theme of women's motivations throughout the Revolution. The winter months of 1793 were no exception. The women had been meeting, along with their husbands, in the club originally founded by Claude Dansard, in a room in the cellar of the Jacobin convent. They had struggled there to understand the broader problems of the Revolution, and to deal with their own familial problems, the most urgent of which concerned food supply and hunger. It has been said that it was here in the evenings in this cellar that the women could be seen in full politcal action.[3] Months before the women put forward the request for their own club, Marat, in *L'Ami du peuple,* praised the women for their subterranean assemblies which Providence, he said, seemed to have placed underneath the Jacobin Club "in order to repair [the club's] mistakes."[4]

On the twenty-fourth of February several groups of women arrived at the Convention and requested admission to the bar. Led by the Citizeness Wafflard, vice-president of the group which met in the Jacobin cellar, the women explained their presence and intentions. Wafflard let it be known that as mothers and wives of the "defenders of the *patrie*" and due to their concern with the scarcity of the basic necessities of life, they had come to express to the Assembly the anger which overwhelmed them.[5] On the same day a group of laundresses also complained before the Convention that the head of a tyrant had fallen under the blade of the law, but now the blade was weighing on the heads of the public bloodsuckers who claimed to be friends but who caressed the people "only in order to better suffocate it."[6]

In May, 1793 the women appeared before the Paris Commune with their official request to form a women's club. *Le Moniteur* reported that the goal of the society would be to thwart the projects of the enemies of the Republic. The meeting place of the society would be the library of the Jacobins on Rue St. Honoré.[7] The society's charter provided for a new president to be elected every month. The best known of the presidents were Claire Lacombe and Pauline Léon. Although Claire Lacombe has mainly kept her place in history due to her association with the *Citoyennes,* she had been politically aware and active before that affiliation occurred. She was not resident in Paris until April of 1792, having arrived there from Toulon. On 25 July of that year she petitioned the Assembly for the right to serve in the army. She declared her patriotism eloquently and offered her services to her country. She stated that she could not help her country, which had been declared in danger, by means of "material sacrifice" but that she was able to "give the gift of her person." In the same address she declared her hatred of despots and exhorted mothers to make their contribution equal to her own by inculcating in their children "love of liberty and horror of despots." She made a concrete suggestion for improving the country's present military situation; Lafayette, should not be allowed to lead the French armies. His leadership could only be justified by those wishing to undermine the Republic with "infamous projects." She asked why he had not been disciplined. Was the Assembly waiting for enemies of the *patrie* to arrive in the Senate and destroy it with hatchets and fire? She warned that enemies of the nation would soon be in their midst and she encouraged the members of the Assembly to act. She demanded that they "raise themselves to their full heights" and name competent leaders. "Say a word, only a word, and the enemies will disappear."[8] Although her petition was received with the applause due such eloquence, and this was probably due not so much to her patriotism and fiery oratory as to the fact that she was quite beautiful, her request for employment was not granted. *Le Moniteur* made little of her eloquent address. On 28 July it reported that "a young citizeness had just offered her person for combat against the enemies of the *patrie.*"[9]

Claire Lacombe participated in the insurrection at the Tuileries on 10 August, 1792, and received a civic crown for her efforts. On the twenty-fifth she thanked the Legislative Assembly for this crown which had been offered to her by the *fédérés* (citizen soldiers from the provinces) along with a tricolour belt and a certificate which bore witness to the fact of her courage on the tenth of August. This was accompanied by honourable mention in the Assembly.[10] The certificate that accompanied the award stated that that she had fought the "satellites of a perfidious court" and that by her courage and her bravery, "little common to her sex," she had rallied the populace.[11]

At the beginning of April, 1793, after the defection of the French General Dumouriez to the Austrians, Claire Lacombe proposed to the Jacobins that the aristocrats of Paris and their families should be

French Woman Armed for Combat. (Artist's conception). Courtesy Musée Carnavalet

seized as hostages.[12]   Her belief in direct action in matters of importance was obvious. At about this same time the *Société des Citoyennes Républicaines Révolutionnaires* was beginning to take shape. Exactly how Lacombe became president is uncertain. It is known that the Citizeness Lecointre led groups which petitioned the Jacobins and the Assembly during the spring. It was not until 26 June that Claire Lacombe appeared at the head of a delegation. The society's petition of 26 August to the Convention was signed by Citizeness Champion, president. It is certain that Claire Lacombe did not succeed to the presidency before September and in the short period remaining before the prohibition of the clubs on 30 October she made a name for herself as a gifted speaker and a person possessing intellect and reason.

Immediately after Lacombe's term in office came the presidency of Pauline Léon, who was also a person of talent and intelligence. Like her predecessor she had a history of political involvement which preceded the *Citoyennes*. She had been active on 14 July, 1789 helping to barricade the streets and to offer encouragement and assistance wherever she could.[13]   She was known for her hatred of Lafayette whom she regarded as a traitor after the October Days. Léon was at the Champ de Mars on 17 July, 1791 in order to sign the petition demanding the dethronement of the king, and she witnessed the massacre which took place there. Later she was beaten up, mistreated by neighbours, and even threatened with prison for her political beliefs and activities.

March 6, 1792 saw Léon at the Assembly at the head of a group of women who were petitioning to "reclaim for all the right to defend one's life and liberty." She questioned what was to become of women if their fathers, brothers, husbands, died at the hands of the enemy. "Can it be forbidden to us either to avenge them or to die at their sides?" She reminded the Assembly that women were citizens and she stressed that the deputies should bear in mind that their predecessors had put the sacred trust of the Constitution into women's hands as well as into their own. She queried how this sacred trust was to be saved if women did not have the arms to defend it from the attacks of its enemies. She explained that the women felt that they needed to have weapons and they had come to request permission to get them.

> You are not able to refuse us and society is not able to take away this right which nature has given to us, unless it can be claimed that the Declaration of Rights does not apply to women and that we must allow our throats to be slit like lambs without having the right to defend ourselves because we believe that the tyrants will spare us.[14]

If the enemy is victorious, should women be condemned to wait in their homes for a horrible death and all the horrors that would precede it? Perhaps, declared Léon, women would suffer an even worse misfortune, that of surviving after all they have held most dear, their families and their liberty, has been destroyed. The petition emphasized that women wanted to obtain weapons, wished permission to practise military manœuvres on Sundays and holidays, and asked to have as their commander a member of the National Guard, always, of course, "in compliance with the rules that the wisdom of Monsieur the Mayor has prescribed for the good order and public tranquillity." This could not be interpreted as merely a simple request to the Assembly for the means to participate militarily. This was a declaration of equality. The request was for arms in the short run because war was imminent and defeat a very real possibility, but at the heart of this address was the desire to play an active role in public affairs. The fact that Pauline Léon read the petition was an indication of the political role she would soon play as member and president of the *Citoyennes*. Later the same year Léon did in fact take up arms, not against an external foe but against King Louis XVI, for she, like Lacombe, was among the insurgents of August 10, 1792. She offered her pike, however, to an unarmed *sans-culotte* whom she admonished to use it well. Léon later signed an address demanding the death of the king and her name graced many patriotic petitions.[15]

The society never had a large membership. It is said to have had about one hundred seventy members maximum,[16] with about one hundred who regularly attended the meetings. Of the nine members for whom the ages are known, six were relatively young, between the ages of twenty-five and thirty years. The other third were between the ages of sixty and seventy, and although there are no surviving minutes of the meetings, some detailed information on how the club functioned does exist. Article 13 of the Statute stated that any woman wishing to become a member of the society must be presented by one woman and supported by two others. Their names would be announced in the next meeting and posted. The women would be admitted if there were no objections. If there were objections their admissions would be postponed. Objections would be heard by the Committee of Correspondence which would make its report to the society. The society would then, "in its wisdom," judge the denunciations. As well, every new citizen would be required by the President, in the name of the society, to take the oath as follows: "I swear to live for the Republic or to die for it; I promise to be faithful to the rules of the Society, as long as it exists." Article 26 stated that since the society granted all its members the right to speak, and since young members might, with the best intentions, compromise the Society with frivolous motions, a minimum age for admission would be established as eighteen years. Mothers could bring their children with them up to age eighteen but they would not have a voice in debates. The society would have three committees, each one composed of a dozen members. As well as the Committee of Correspondence, there would be a committee of administration and a committee of welfare. The possession of "good morals" was the "most essential" condition for admission. As well, the president was to wear the red hat of the Revolution.[17]

The actual objectives of the club are best revealed not just in its oath, in promising to live or to die for the *patrie* but also in its petition to the Jacobins of 12 May, 1793. At this time the women requested that they be allowed to arm in order to fight "the enemies within." They stated, "We have resolved to guard the interior just as our brothers will guard the borders."[18] The women viewed the defence of the *patrie* as a dual undertaking and they divided revolutionary responsibilities accordingly. The men were responsible for defence on the exterior; that is, for winning the foreign wars. The women, on the other hand, would look to safeguarding the Revolution in the interior, being ever on the alert against counter-revolutionary threats. This was the premise from which the *Citoyennes* began their activities. Their attempts to carry our this responsiblity as they conceived it became increasingly violent as the Revolution progressed. Their presence at the Jacobin Club on 12 May announced their intentions.

A delegation of the *Société des Républicaines Révolutionnaires,* meeting at the library of the Jacobins, was introduced. The spokesman for the delegation said that the Society proposes to arm women patriots between the ages of eighteen and fifty years and to organize them in army units against the Vendée. The President welcomed the delegation.[19]

The presentation was much more involved and patriotic than this brief report would suggest. The women demanded the extermination of villains, the arrest of all traitors, and the formation of "companies of amazons." They announced that they had resolved to guard the interior because the men would be at the frontiers and they had sworn "to perish under the smoking ruins of this city rather than to capitulate to the conquerors."[20] In the same presentation they called for a harsh tax on wealth in order to assure subsistence levels for the wives of soldiers and they invited all the women to sign their petition because they loved only those "of whom the heart glows with the fire of patriotism." The petition proclaimed that these women would save the country and that there should be no attempts to discourage them.[21] On 19 May the women of the *Citoyennes* teamed up with members of the *Club des Cordeliers* and appeared once again at the Jacobin Club. The spokesperson announced a petition composed by members of both societies and then proceeded to read it to the assembly. It opened with a warning that the *patrie* was in the most imminent danger and stated that if there was a desire to save it, the most vigorous measures would be necessary. In the uproar which followed the orator was forced to call for order and attention. He, or possibly she, succeeded in regaining control and proceeded to warn that there were conspirators waiting in the wings to burn patriots and all that they held dear as soon as the volunteers had left for the Vendée.

In order to prevent these horrible events, it should be decreed immediately that suspects would be arrested and that there would be established revolutionary tribunals in all the departments and sections of Paris.[22]

Next came the accusations against certain of the Girondins that have served to lead some historians to conclude that the sole purpose of the *Citoyennes* was to overthrow that group in the Convention. The spokesperson proclaimed that for a long time several of the leading Girondin personalities have been designated as the ringleaders of the army of the counter-revolutionaries and asked why they had not been formally accused, stating that criminals are nowhere sacred.[23] Furthermore, the speaker asked for the establishment in each city of revolutionary armies composed of *sans-culottes* in proportion to their population and that the army of Paris be increased to forty thousand men to be paid by the rich. They proposed that all public places should become workshops where iron would be converted into arms of all types. There existed, according to the speaker, a terrible plot to make the people die of starvation by keeping essential food items at enormous prices. It was necessary for the legislators to hit the hoarders, the carpetbaggers, and the "egoïste" merchants. All should be exterminated and the *patrie* would be wealthy with the "virtues of the *sans-culottes.*" The speaker then implored the audience to come to the rescue of all the unfortunates. "It is the cry of Nature. It is the vow of true patriots. Our heart is torn by the spectacle of public misery." The goal of the group, it was stated, was to resurrect man from his state of misery and have not one unfortunate remaining in the Republic. This address, concluded the speaker, must be taken to the Convention. There it would be determined if enemies within would dare to oppose measures proposed for the good of the Republic.[24]

To all this the President of the Jacobins, at this time Bentabole, replied that "the Society hears with the utmost satisfaction these most pure and ardent expressions of patriotism..... The Society supports your efforts with all its courage because it has the same principles and it has expressed the same opinions."[25] The next day the joint deputation arrived at the Council of the Paris Commune and the President congratulated the women on their "male energy" and invited them to the meeting.[26]

One week later, 27 May, the women sent a new deputation to the Jacobins. This time there were no men included. The spokeperson was the Citizeness Lecointre. It was reported with brevity that

> ...the Citizeness Lecointre, speaking in the name of a delegation of *La Société des Républicaines Révolutionnaires,* affirmed that her companions are not 'servile women' or 'domestic animals.' Rather, they will form a phalanx whose purpose it will be to annihilate the aristocrats. The president welcomed them; then he declared that the meeting was over.[27]

THE *CITOYENNES* AGAINST THE GIRONDINS

From shortly after its formal organization on 10 May, the *Citoyennes* began to involve itself in the greatest political issue then dividing the National Convention and the city of Paris, the struggle for dominance between the rival factions of the Jacobins and the Girondins. Some of the city's forty-eight sections were circulating petitions demanding the removal of twenty-two Girondin deputies and on 13 May a police spy reported that the women of the *Citoyennes* "persevered in demanding the removal of the twenty-two deputies.

They [the women] even hoped that they would be supported by the men."[28]   At the same time, the *Citoyennes* became involved in a political struggle over the seating arrangements in the public galleries of the National Convention. The women were opposing decrees of the Convention, presumably adopted through Girondin influence, that authorized the deputies to distribute four hundred tickets to their friends. The women demanded to be admitted to the galleries along with the friends of the deputies who carried passes. The Assembly heard their complaints, then passed immediately on to the business of the day. In its next meeting the members of the *Citoyennes* determined to put a stop to such discrimination. From nine a.m. they stood guard at the door of the Convention and stopped anyone with passes from entering. Police reported that crowds of women were harassing citizens trying to enter the public galleries; they tore up tickets of men they called Girondins and Brissotins.[29]   The result was "a type of riot caused by women." One of these was arrested and when National Guardsmen took her away she was followed by a female crowd who protested in her defence.[30]   It was in this kind of situation that Théroigne de Méricourt on 15 May was assaulted by a group of spectators and publicly humiliated, after which her brief political career came to an end.[31]

At about the same time women began to interrupt proceedings within the Convention. They caused disturbances in the corridors and the noise upset the deputies in the Salle de Séances. On 18 May, Isnard, the Girondin president of the Convention, rose and issued a warning to the deputies, prefacing his remarks with the declaration that

> ...if you were able to open my heart, you would see my love for my country; and if I were to be burned in this chair, my last sigh would be only for my country, and my last words; 'God, pardon my assassins, they are lost; but save the liberty of my country.'[32]

He went on to say that enemies of the Republic wished, by force of troubles and disorders, to put one section against the other, and to cause an uprising among the people. He predicted that the insurrection would begin with the women who wished to dissolve the Convention. The English would then capitalize on this moment to descend on France and then a counter-revolution would be underway. On the same day, Gamon, another Girondin who was a member of a committee responsible for inspecting the premises, rose in the Convention to complain about the women's activities. He said that the inspectors had received complaints every day since the Convention began meeting in this new room from several deputies and citizens of various departments. They complained that the women were playing police at the doors of the tribunes of the Convention and they were tearing up tickets and insulting and threatening those attempting to enter there.[33] He reported that several of these women had been brought before the committee and they had declared that they met at the Jacobins "under the title of the Women of the Fraternity." One had testified that "the Convention has established a despotism with regard to what places in the galleries are allotted through tickets to the citizens of our departments" and stated that it was necessary to oppose that. The women also explained that the society had decreed that they would stop the use of such passes to obtain seats in the galleries. The women had declared that since the beginning of the week they had been working steadily to implement this decree. Gamon went on to explain that he had pointed out the errors in their reasoning and conduct but without results. He told them that they were guilty of opposing the implementation of a law and that their conduct had to be the result of error or perfidious suggestions. He stated that he had explained that it was unjust to deprive the citizens of the departments of the opportunity to observe the meetings and enjoined the group to conform to the law and to respect public opinion.[34]

Deputy Gamon also had some comments about the situation of the women. He said that he had observed that these women "who regularly disturb our meetings" were obviously paid by enemies of the Republic. "In reality," he said, "almost all of them carry the stamp of misery; they do not appear to have any other means of known support than their daily work." The women, he observed, passed their days in the corridors and distributed themselves in such a way as to sit in the doors of the galleries. He complained that these women were not without seats and that they could have observed the meetings peacefully, but that they preferred, however, to "maintain disorder." They obstinately blocked the door of each gallery to those with passes and Gamon stated that he had to attribute their behaviour to aristocrats and anarchists. He closed his address with the hope that these "lost women" would not continue to serve the enemies of liberty. In response the Montagnard deputy, Ruhl, stated that "equality exists everywhere" and if passes to the galleries were suppressed the women would no longer have this pretext for coming there and they would cease to do so. Isnard then spoke again on the topic of the women's behaviour. He said that a citizen whom he had named to the Committee of General Security had asked these women why they were blocking the galleries without reason. He claimed that their response indicated that they were being paid to do it.[35]   The Girondin, Buzot, was of the same opinion. On 20 May he complained that the problem with the women had not been solved despite two decrees. "It is essential that the galleries be equally accessible to all citizens and not just to aggressive women, avid of murder and of blood, who will push the most ferocious principles in depraved societies." He then proposed that the passes to the sittings of the Convention would be distributed in the sections of the city by the section presidents at the general meetings.[36]

On the same day, when the Girondin deputy from Marseilles was speaking, voices from the galleries shouted "Down with Barbaroux." He descended from the tribune and was succeeded by Larivière, a Girondin deputy from Calvados, who demanded that the meeting be adjourned "in the observance of the default of liberty."[37]   The next speaker was Marat who asked the meaning of the "panic terror" which surrounded them.[38]   On 22 May the police spy, Dutard, referred to "the heroines of liberty," meaning the members of the *Citoyennes*, of whom he said that he had seen about a dozen on the terrace of the Tuileries the evening before. They were, he said, engaged in a very lively discussion with a deputy of the Convention. This was taking place at the door of the Convention where the women were blocking anyone who had passes delivered by the deputies. Dutard described the women as probably the concubines of the Jacobins or else paid by the Jacobins. He was of the opinion that the National Guard had only to resist them with "prudence and reason" and they would not attempt anything.[39]

Although Dutard seems to have misinterpreted the will of the women, who were very serious in their determination to unseat the Girondins, he nonetheless noted a demonstration protesting the imprisonment of the Montagnard, Hébert, editor of *Le Père Duchesne.* Dutard reported that shouts arose on all sides and that the women were in battle formation with a flag on display. They were moving in the direction of the Pont Neuf and they invited passersby to go with them to the Abbaye Prison to free *le père Duchesne,* who had been arrested by the Committee of Twelve at the inspiration of the Girondins. The women were in a violent frame of mind, according to the report. "These excellent patriots had pikes in their hands, swords, or big knives. They shouted, 'Down with the Committee of Twelve! Long live the Mountain! To the guillotine with the Brissotins! Long live Marat! Long live Father Duchesne!' " Dutard reported as well a fracas on the terrace of the Tuileries where a deputy who had been intercepted by the women asked them who had given them permission to be there. The response from one of them was as follows: "Equality. Are we not all equal? And if we are all equal, I have the right to enter just as much as those who have the cards." When threatened with expulsion, the woman responded, "Go, Monsieur, this is not your place, your place is in the meeting room, and in spite of all your efforts, we will stay here and we will work on your sins."[40]

The women did not confine their activities to the Convention. They were involved in confrontations in other places as well. In the section meeting the women, who in normal times were merely spectators, took sides in the pro-Montagnard versus pro-Girondin disputes and at times were wounded in the *mêlées* when objects such as chairs were thrown at their heads. One such encounter took place on the evening of 22 May in the section of Butte-des-Moulins where a crowd of one hundred to one hundred-fifty women and some men confronted moderates of the section where petitions from the *Club des Cordeliers* and the *Citoyennes* had twice been ignored. On 29 May the women of the section Mont Blanc were forbidden to observe the meetings of the general assembly. This was instigated by the section president, Fielval, who was considered to be an aristocrat *gangrené* by the women of the *Citoyennes.* The pretext used for the exclusion was the size of the room, but the women knew that the real reason was their support of the *sans-culottes.* The women employed the same methods at the door of the section assembly as they did at the door of the Convention. A dozen of them were posted at the door of the meeting room asking each person wishing admittance if he were an aristocrat. When the president was leaving the women attacked him, insulting him in "a most outrageous manner," threatening to rip off his epaulettes, and even to hang him.[41]

Another police spy, Perrière, left little doubt that in his opinion the women were a force to be recognized. They were, he said, determined, serious, and bold in their intentions. On 27 May he wrote that following report:

> I have heard that there were a considerable number of meetings last evening at the Tuileries, at the Jacobins, and in the Faubourg Saint-Antoine. The one at the Tuileries consisted especially of women put politically in the forefront by the men who did not dare themselves to attempt a *coup* .[42]

The same policeman stated that the Girondins were the target of the women's wrath. He said of the women that they were thirsty and "it was particularly from the skulls of Buzot, Brissot, and their friends that they wished to drink."

La Patriote française, also on 27 May, 1793 described the women's activities.

> Last evening, these women rose together [in a demonstration]; they displayed a beautiful banner and a beautiful red bonnet; they sang the litanies of Marat while awaiting the requiem of the Brissotins. They hoped to produce a general insurrection of the men, but none joined in. The women withdrew but the whole thing has resumed today.[43]

Further evidence that the women were increasingly active in the days preceding the fall of the Girondins is found in Gorsas' *Le Courrier des 83 departements* which reported on 28 May that the women who call themselves revolutionary gathered together, and circulated, shrieking, in the streets. Gorsas described the women as screaming like bacchantes ready to tear the limbs from Orpheus. He said that they had, on the previous Sunday, spread throughout the districts of the city with weapons in one hand and the standard of revolt in the other.[44] The women were gathering for insurrection and "a subversive agitation" reigned in Paris with the women being in the process of arming themselves with pistols and daggers. They were appearing, he said, in all parts of the city, "carrying the standard of licence." They wished "to purge the Convention, make heads fall, and get themselves drunk on blood."[45]

The women were indeed active in the insurrection that they had helped prepare. They held their places and participated with energy and dedication in the days that followed. Determined and serious in their desire to unseat the Girondins, the citizenesses made their presence felt from 31 May to 2 June and beyond. In the last days of May they joined with the radical Jacobins, led by Hébert, now released from prison, and his partner, Varlet, to form a revolutionary committee of the sections. This group met in the former bishop's palace, the Evêché, and lent support to the Committee of the Insurrectionary Commune which was also directed by Hébert along with Pache, the mayor of Paris, and Chaumette. The two committees, with the women of the *Citoyennes* in the very vanguard of the action, requested volunteers for the insurgent National Guard, attempted to oust all moderates from section committees, and called for a purge of all former clergy and nobility from the government bureaucracies. Not the least of the demands requested a general maximum or price ceiling on basic necessities. The Girondins were well aware that they were the first targets of the women's discontent.[46]

At three a.m. on the morning of 31 May the drum sounded from the headquarters at the Evêché. About a hundred women are said to have been present at this location during the night.[47] The representatives of each section gathered at the Hôtel de Ville in conference with the General Council of the Paris Commune. Delegates of the *Citoyennes* sought to participate in the planning of the insurrection, but were permitted only as observers. *Le Moniteur* of 2 June reported that a deputation from the *Citoyennes* presented itself to the Council and demanded to be admitted to the deliberations of the male *comité révolutionnaire*. The response was less than gratifying.

> The council congratulates the citizens on their republican zeal and extends to them their regrets that they are not able to admit them to the Men's Revolutionary Committee. This committee is not a club but is composed of deputies from the forty-eight sections. The women are invited to observe the meetings.[48]

This event seems to have entirely escaped the notice of historians .[49]

The tribunes of the Convention were crowded with women on 31 May and they were vociferous and loud in their demands. They heckled the reporter for the *Commission des Douze* (created by the Girondins to investigate *sans-culottes'* activities in Paris) and expressed support for the deputation from the sections demanding the exclusion of the Girondins from the proceedings and the implementation of social and economic programs to help the *sans-culottes.* In the streets the women supported the insurgents. One instance is recorded of a woman of sixty-two years threatening to stab the National Guards who were trying to rejoin their comrades. It is reported that she said the knife that she had drawn from her pocket was as much for them as for the aristocrats because that is what they also were.[50] She was arrested and later released thanks to a deputation from the *Citoyennes* led by one Constance Evrard, to whom the police granted custody of the woman.

The next day, 1 June, was a quieter day but the women observed the meeting of the Commune and at one point suggested that the brave *sans-culottes* volunteers be provided with necessities so that they would be able to remain at their posts. The Council of the Commune agreed and ordered the sections to send wagons full of foodstuffs to the battalions.[51] On 2 June when the movement to unseat the Girondins accelerated, and the insurrectional committee had the National Guard surround the Convention, the women went inside as part of a delegation from the sections. Apparently they presented their own petition but the content is not known.[52]

Eyewitness accounts of the women's role on 2 June are scarce but the Girondin Gorsas afterwards declared that the men who tried to stop the proscribed Girondins from escaping the Manège were assisted by "a troop of women calling themselves revolutionaries, a troop of *furies,* avid of carnage." He reported that the women were armed and these "shameless" females held the deputies captive. It appeared that one of the Girondins, "followed by five or six of these shrews," was forced to jump in a ditch in order to escape them.[53] The same day a young woman arrested in the courtyard of the Convention was said to be armed with daggers and with pistols.[54]

The Girondin, Buzot, writing of that day in his *Mémoires,* depicted the women as having played a major role in the events. He said that an old reprobate of Paris (female, of course) commanded the women and their daggers belonged to whoever could best pay them. He believed that Claire Lacombe was their leader and that she had a large following, *"un grand empire."* He stated that in the split between the Robespierrist and Dantonist factions Claire Lacombe would be able to tip the balance in favour of the side that she supported. He questioned the "excess of infamy" to which the French people had been driven. Buzot emphasized that if the Girondins had been counter-revolutionnaries they would have been accepted by the Jacobins and the women's club due to "perfidy, baseness, and crime." He added that in that case, surrounded by all that is the most despicable and corrupt in humanity, the Girondins would have publicly or in secret responded appropriately by getting rid of all of them.[55] But from the side of the victors in the insurrection, Jacques Roux, before the General Council of the Commune, praised the *Citoyennes* for sharing "the glory of having saved the Republic in the days between 31 May and 2 June."[56]

In July, 1793 the citizenesses of the Section of the Droits de l'Homme presented the *Citoyennes* with a flag on which was written the Declaration of the Rights of Man and Citizen. The address given at that time congratulated the members of the society for their part in bringing about the fall of the Girondins. They were praised for their efforts to change women's place in society.

> You have broken the rings in the chain of prejudices. They no longer exist for you, the things that have relegated you to the narrow sphere of the household. You wish to hold your place in the social order, neutrality offends and humiliates you....Liberty smiles on your commendable aspirations. She sees in them the most favorable omen. Already she saw you under the banner propagating these principles. Your apostolic missions prepared the memorable revolution of 31 May....Your mission was delicate. There were proprieties to observe and your zeal, appropriately controlled, facilitated our success. Courage, perseverance, brave Republicans![57]

The evidence shows that the women of the *Citoyennes* were indeed in the vanguard of the insurrection. It shows, in fact, that during the spring of 1793 the women were among the most active elements in the revolutionary movement. They agitated for and prepared the insurrection and participated in it in the Convention, the Commune, the sections, and on the streets. Many of the women who became involved, who sat in the galleries of the Convention and attended the section meetings, were not actually club members, but rather women who had responded to the call from the club and in rallying around the club standard had received the encouragement and support they needed to participate actively in the political life of the new nation.

THE SUMMER OF '93

During the summer of 1793 the women of the *Citoyennes* reached the height of their influence, their "days of glory," in which they participated with enthusiasm and determination in the political life of the nation. Those few weeks which followed the insurrection of 31 May-2 June were halcyon days for the women of the *Citoyennes*. In the celebrations marking the completion of the Montagnard Constitution on 23 June, 1793 club members had a place of prominence. Their procession circled the altar of the *patrie* as the women sang hymns of praise to liberty. The next day in the Convention, the artist-deputy David, paid homage to the women. He said that at the Champ-de-Mars it was these women, "true Republicans" and mothers of families who, by their example "gave to their children the first lessons in virtue." Women, he stated, had been revered and applauded during the celebration. "Three times the women circled the altar of the *patrie* and three times the people responded to this performance so dear to its heart."[58] The minutes of the general assembly of the forty-eight sections recorded on 30 June that "in the civil ceremony of which they [the women] were the attraction, they employed all the power they had over the citizens to inspire their courage and to press them to fly to fight the rebels."[59]

A longer letter from the same source, signed by Louis Pierre Dufourny, president of the Commune, was sent to the *Citoyennes* and stated that the women had served their country well, "their zeal being indefatigable, their surveillance penetrating conspiracies, their activities thwarting them, their defiance brushing them aside, their audacity foreseeing the dangers and their courage surmounting them." These women did not wish to be slaves but wanted the esteem of

L' action . Les premiers conflits

Républicaines participant à une réunion d'un des clubs patriotiques de femmes. (Frères Lesueur. Musée Carnavalet.)

Meeting of a Patriotic Women's Club. P.E. LeSueur. Courtesy Musée Carnavalet

men who were themselves free. They were "wives and republicans, their hearths not able to contain the abundance of their affections." They sacrificed their pleasures for their country, they armed their spouses and their children. The list of the virtues of the women was quite lengthy. "They repulsed humiliations, they remained faithful to the oaths they had taken, they pursued and struggled with traitors, they scorned adornment....Their dances surround the altar, all their songs celebrate liberty, and their most ardent raptures are for the Republic." The participation, wisdom, and generosity of the women, in the eyes of their admirers, were boundless.

These heroines who fought at the Bastille, who went to Versailles, who had to avenge their spouses and their children sacrificed on the altar of the *patrie*, and who finally overwhelmed the Swiss and tyranny, became just as prudent as they were courageous, and resisted all insidious suggestions.[60]

According to this source, in the events of 31 May-2 June the women recognized that "men of blood" were wishing to use them to give the signal for civil war. They trembled at the plague of civil war which crushed only half of the human race but spread also to the other half. They disdained ultimately the power of force and had exercised only the power of persuasion. As well, they had taken over the doors and the seats in the Convention, maintained egality, intimidated the traitors, and largely prepared the insurrection. Although the enormous problems facing the Convention had impeded its ability to construct the Constitution, the women, with their "tender solicitude" had helped it recover and function effectively so that it was capable of completing its task. Could these virtuous creatures have been the same as those in the reports of the Girondins? Apparently so, but in this account of their activities they were praised for their activities amongst the people. The letter also reminded them of their continuing responsibilities, to "excite zeal" and "rejuvenate hard work" and to remind family members of their responsibilities and rights. In this way the *patrie* would be saved.[61]

Opinions vary as to who the women were that comprised the membership of the *Citoyennes*. In his memoirs, one of the Girondins, Buzot, claimed that these women were "lost women," who had been "picked up from the filth of the capital, of whom the boldness equalled only the impudence, female monsters who have all the cruelty of weakness and all the vices of their sex."[62] Other hostile contemporaries called them "public women," "unfortunates paid twenty cents per day," and "termagants without shame."[63] Perhaps worst of all, and adding insult to injury, the women were accused of being ugly. It was said that they were *toutes laides à faire peur* or ugly enough to be frightening[64] and that they were heads of Medusa, "the aspect of who would petrify."[65] But ugliness was obviously not a prerequisite for membership, because both Claire Lacombe and Pauline Léon were reputed to be beautiful.

The club membership was plagued by accusations of immorality and it took action to refute these claims. On 14 September a delegation from the club presented at a meeting of the General Council of the Commune a proposal that they wished to take to the Convention. The purpose was to demand the incarceration of "public women" and female suspects" whose influence could cause the worst misfortunes.[66] They had proposed the same measures the previous day at the Jacobin Club and had been enthusiastically applauded.[67] On 18 September at the evening session of the Convention, the women presented their proposal in an expanded form. They suggested that *les femmes de mauvaise vie* (prostitutes) be transferred to "national houses" and occupied there with useful work. The goal would be to bring them back, if possible, to good morals by means of honest labour and patriotic lectures. The petition referred to "these victims of libertinage, of whom the heart is often good, and that misery alone has almost always reduced to this deplorable state."[68] There were also club rules that emphasized the importance of good morals. In the preamble to the club's charter, the *Citoyennes* proclaimed that "without morals and without principles there is no liberty."[69]

Article 12 emphasized the same qualities, stating that

> ...the Society, being of good moral standing, supports and only encourages in its breast citizenesses of good morals; it has made this condition the most essential for admission and desires that the lack of good morals be made one of the principal causes of exclusion.[70]

Any analysis of the membership of the club by occupation is difficult because there are few documents which are relevant. Apparently there were, besides the actress Claire Lacombe, and the chocolate maker Pauline Léon, two members known to be merchants of dry goods, one printer, and two cake merchants from Nanterre. The former were Justine Thibault, roommate of Claire Lacombe, and the Citizeness Monic. Madame Coulombe was the proprietoress of the printshop of *L'Ami du peuple.* There were also included in the membership a former hat seller, a meat seller, a laundress, a seamstress, two table linen workers, the wife of a pipefitter, a polisher, a shoemaker, two cooks, and the wife of a harness-maker.[71] It appears that the women, although not highly educated, were capable for the most part of reading and writing. Only seven of twenty-two women for whom this information is available could not sign their names. It is necessary to note, however, that most of the women for whom information is available were the club's officials. The educational level of the simple members would be impossible to determine with accuracy.[72]

At the end of July or the beginning of August the club moved its meetings from the library of the Jacobin convent to the charnel houses of Saint-Eustache and this was to be its meeting place until its demise at the end of October. Women who were not members could observe the meetings if they were recommended by two members.

The society wished to maintain ties with other revolutionary societies and over the months asked for affiliation with various other clubs
in Paris. A contemporary source offers a rare and fascinating if bi-
ased account of a meeting of the *Citoyennes* dating from early August, 1793.[73] P. J. A. Roussel, who wrote under the name Prousinalle,
said that he attended the meeting because he was curious to learn
about the women and their concerns and activities. The president
and secretaries faced the door, the sixty-six members sat on two rows
of benches on each side facing the officials. The observer declared
that "this grotesque spectacle almost caused us to suffocate from the
constraint required for us not to burst out laughing." First, the president introduced the evening's topic which was to be a discussion of
women's usefulness to a republican government. She asked those
who had done research on the topic to speak. Citizeness Monic took
up the challenge and appears to have given a rousing recital, complete with historic allusions. "Women must form batallions, command armies, fight and conquer just like men. If anyone still wishes
to doubt it, I would cite Pantée, Ingonde, Clothild, Isabelle, Marguerite." And she asked the men believing themselves to be the masters
of women, who it was that delivered Judea and Syria from the
Holofernes? It was Judith, a woman. She declared that Rome owes
its liberty and Republic to two women.[74]

The speaker next applauded the performance of women in the
Revolution, both at the Bastille and at Versailles. "At the siege of the
Bastille women who had previously seen only fireworks were exposed to the cannons and the artillery on the ramparts, in order to
bring ammunition to the assailants." In October, 1789, "It was a
battalion of women, commanded by the brave Reine Audu, who went

to search for the despot at Versailles, and brought him in triumph to Paris, after having fought and disarmed the bodyguards." She then included the feats of the club's president, Claire Lacombe, on the tenth of August. "She marched valiantly against the Chateau, at the head of a group of soldiers. She carries still the marks of that day." Citizeness Monic then alluded to those women who had "governed with glory," naming, among others, Isabelle of Spain, Catherine of Russia, and Catherine de Medici. She concluded with a request that "the society in its wisdom examine the place that women must occupy in the Republic and whether it is necessary to continue to exclude them from all posts and administrations."[75] During this meeting at least, the emphasis lay with encouraging women to participate, on bolstering their courage and self-esteem, and convincing them that women do possess attributes necessary for meaningful political participation. Citizeness Monic's presentation was met with almost frenetic approval. "This discourse, often interrupted, ended with a crown of violent applause."[76]

The caustic comments of Roussel are worth noting. "Nothing appears more comical to us than hearing passages of history delivered by a woman who murders all the words with an assurance difficult to describe." He stated that the applause was accompanied by a long murmur followed in turn by propositions which were "each one more ridiculous than the others." One suggestion involved an army of thirty thousand women to fight the enemy and in which all the "public women" would be forced to march. Another suggestion, regarded as utterly ridiculous by the observer, was that women be admitted to serve in all areas of government administration.[77]

Next at the tribune during this meeting was Olympe de Gouges, the colourful revolutionary figure who became famous for the use of the written word as her weapon. Highly skilled orator and writer that she was, she carried out a lively crusade throughout the Revolution aimed at improving the situation of women in society. Her best known work was her Declaration of the Rights of Woman, previously mentioned, in which she declared that women, having the right to mount the scaffold, should have equally the right to mount the tribune. Ironically, she was to be executed during the Terror. During her lifetime she was never affiliated with any specific club, but she obviously felt it was worthwhile to express her ideas before a group of women with some type of organized political objectives. She is reported to have stated that "Man in isolation is our slave. It is only when grouped together that they crush us with their arrogance. The greatest fault that our sex has committed has been to submit to this demeaning custom, which makes man totally superior." Women, she stated, should only marry men who would be willing to fight for their countries. If the man in question was not in agreement, she had a solution. He should hear these words: "Stay, fainthearted soul, but never think that you will be united with your lover for she has sworn to reject the promises of a man useless to his country." She added that women should demand to direct celebrations, marriages, and education of the young. They would replace existing institutions and start a religion "of true *sans-culottes*."[78]

Roussel's mocking description of the *Citoyennes* obviously fails to do it justice, for the club was a far more serious political entity than he cared to indicate. It was not without its problems, however, and these were not always the result of male attitudes. As could be expected during a time of such great change, all elements of the female population did not always act together in harmony. Even the club membership became polarized in their revolutionary efforts, and there existed many factions within the broader female population, exclusive of the club, which held their own views on the revolutionary situation. As we have observed, Théroigne de Méricourt, as a supporter of the Girondins, was publicly humiliated for her opposition to the political views of the women of the *Citoyennes* . There was also the situation with the women of Les Halles. Although the market women recognized the need for change, they despised the Revolution, protested the persecution of the priests, and interacted violently with the women who wore the red bonnets of the *Citoyennes.* They were regarded by some as *aristocrates* and were said to be as much a threat to the Convention in their own way as the members of the *Citoyennes* were in theirs. As the summer progressed the polarization of the women became more and more extreme. The membership of the *Citoyennes*, seething with a need to improve its plight, and the *aristocrates* of the marketplace, many of whom had ties to the old order, exhibited a growing animosity toward one another. The spirit of free enterprise that dominated the market clashed resoundingly with the demands of the women of the *Citoyennes* for economic controls.

Even though the Girondins had been removed from power, the scarcity of the basic necessities of life remained. From the middle of June onward the women of Paris expressed their discontent with the standard of living forced upon them. The rumours of hoarding had not been stilled and the women advocated stringent punishments for this offence. The "red priest," Jacques Roux, a leader of the faction of the *enragés,* an ultra-Jacobin party of the left, for whom women of the *Citoyennes* often expressed sympathy, addressed the Convention on 25 June with a request for a regulated economy because, he said, "Liberty is only a vain phantom when one class of men is able to starve another with impunity. Equality is only a vain phantom when the rich, by monopoly, hold the right of life and death over its own kind." He questioned whether the Convention had taken any steps at all to alleviate the worsening economic situation and emphasized the misery pervasive among the people. Roux was chased from the Convention by the enraged Jacobins, with the deputy Legendre proclaiming that "There are patriots in his section who will mete out justice themselves."[79]

The same day that Jacques Roux incensed the deputies with his call for action on the economic front, groups of women chose to act out their frustration in the streets of Paris. That afternoon a group of laundry women stopped two wagons loaded with soap on the Rue Saint Lazare. The women believed that the merchandise was destined for hoarders and they were determined to stop its delivery. They imposed *taxation populaire* (price fixing) on the spot, decreeing the price of soap to be twenty *sols* per *livre*. Their actions marked the beginning of three days of rioting in the streets of Paris. Despite the fact that the women of the *Citoyennes* had growing reservations about the unwillingness of the Jacobin Convention to act for the good of the people, they did not participate in the riots of these days but rather attempted to calm the women as they expressed their frustrations in the streets of the capital. The minutes of the Paris Commune for 27 June report that a deputation of the *Société des Républicaines Révolutionnaires* informed the committee that they had on this day retrieved several "lost" women from their erroneous ways.[80] The next day the trouble started again and spread to other sections. Rumour had it that the boats arriving in the Paris ports would have to return to Rouen with cargo intact. At six a.m. the women gathered at the bridges Royal and Carousel and distributed soap at the newly fixed price. The Montagnard, Couthon, described the situation to the deputies in the Convention as follows:

> It is very certain that last evening the news was spread that some boatloads of soap, coming from Rouen, were returning to that city....The troublemakers soon spread the word that it was a bureaucratic plot to deprovision Paris and that soon there would arrive no more supplies. The people have been frightened as much as at Evreaux when they had seized several wagons of butter.[81]

Then Couthon directly implicated the women. "Some women, giving in to their fears, went to the vicinity of Grenouillère, where they sold eight cases of soap; from there they went to the Porte St. Nicholas where they did the same thing." He went on to complain that the rioters would not listen to reason and that further measures were necessary. An attempt was made by Commune officials to calm the women but at the same time, in another part of Paris, on the Rue de Provence, a group of women forced a police officer to visit a house where they suspected soap was being hoarded. In the afternoon a group of more than a thousand women confiscated a wagon of soap near the Champs-Elysées.[82]

The rioters were mainly the women of the Parisian working class, exclusive, of course, of the members of the *Citoyennes*.[83] The group included laundresses, merchants from Les Halles, street pedlars, seamstresses, wives of small artisans, bricklayers, and haulers of water. The participants accused the National Guard and passersby of being

hoarders, bourgeois, and aristocrats.[84] They were increasingly afraid
that Paris would be deprived of provisions and famine would result.
After three days the rioting subsided but the precarious position of
the new Jacobin government was by no means secure.

By mid-July the honeymoon of the *Citoyennes* with the Jacobins
was coming to an end. The attitudes of the membership were growing closer to those of the women whom they had termed *égarées*
during the June soap riots. The women of the *Citoyennes* had also
detached themselves from Jacques Roux shortly after his appearance
before the Convention on 24 June. On 13 July Marat was assassinated by Charlotte Corday, a supporter of the Girondins, who had
come to Paris from Caen for the express purpose of killing Marat.
The patriots in the capital mourned Marat in a manner bordering on
the fanatical, the women of the *Citoyennes* not excluded. They felt
that they must in some way compensate for the fact that the "father
of the people" had met his death at the hands of a member of their
sex. The details of his funeral were announced in the Convention on
16 July by David. The report in the *Moniteur* read as follows:

> It had been decreed that his body would be exposed, covered by a wet sheet
> which represented his bathtub, and which, dampened from time to time, stopped
> the effect of putrefaction. It was to be interred that day, at five in the evening,
> under the trees where he had enjoyed teaching his compatriots.[85]

The *Citoyennes* and many supporters turned out in great numbers to
mourn publicly the death of the "people's friend."

The body was displayed at the church of the Cordeliers. On one
side was Marat's bathtub and on the other side was his bloodied shirt.
When the *cortège* left the church for the burial in the garden it took
a very long route and the women took care to mourn noticeably, swear

revenge, throw flowers, and display the tub and shirt to onlookers. The deceased's head had been decorated with a wreath and it was made certain that the wound inflicted by the assassin's knife was visible to onlookers. *Le Courrier universel* reported on 19 July that the *Citoyennes* had sent a deputation to the Convention demanding vengeance for the assassination of Marat. The members swore to follow until death "the enemies of liberty and to imprint on their foreheads the stamp of disgrace."[86] The same day a deputation stated that they planned "to people the earth with children as much like Marat as they were able, that they would raise these children in the cult of Marat, and swear to put in their hands no other learning except the collection of Marat with a poem in his memory, and brand the 'infernal fury fathered by the race of Caen,' " meaning, of course, Charlotte Corday.[87]

On 24 July the *Citoyennes* sent a deputation to the Commune with several requests. The *Moniteur* of 27 July reported that the spokesperson asked that an address be made to the Convention "to invite it to remove the likeness of the last of our tyrants from the assignats." The spokesperson also asked that members of the Convention take action to stop the hoarding of coal. The deputation wished to receive permission to erect a monument to the memory of Marat in front of the Palais National. The Council of the Commune applauded the *civisme* of the women and invited them to the meeting.[88] On 28 July the women participated in the ceremony of the translation of the heart of Marat. Attended by representatives of the Convention, the Commune, and the popular societies, the ceremony saw the heart of the people's idol enclosed in a magnificent vase and placed in the meeting room of the Cordeliers. On 31 July members of the *Citoyennes* again addressed the Commune on the same topic, this time explaining that there was no longer enough time until 10 August when major celebrations were scheduled. The commissaires of the forty-eight sections and the citizens of the popular societies asked to be authorized to erect the obelisk on the Place de la Réunion. The Council authorized them to erect one made of wood provisionally until a more durable one could consecrate the memory of Marat.[89] Permission to erect the obelisk was actually granted to groups other than the *Citoyennes* although it had put the idea forward initially. This was an indication of the rapidly deteriorating relations between the Jacobin Convention and the women's group.

The Jacobin Mountain was supported by the Hébertist Commune and the journal *Père Duchesne,* but the women of the *Citoyennes* were exhibiting a definite tendency to stray from the paths of loyalty to this new government which they had been instrumental in bringing to power. However, as late as 10 August, 1793 the women were the recipients of more praise from the president of the Convention, at the time Hérault de Séchelles, during the Fête of Unity and Indivisibility. "What a spectacle! The weakness of women and the heroism of courage! Oh, Liberty! These are your miracles! It is you who, in these two days when the blood of Versailles began to expiate the crimes of kings, fired in the heart of some women this audacity which has made to flee or fall in front of them these satellites of tyrants." He continued, saying, "Oh, women! Liberty, attacked by all the tyrants, in order to be defended, has need of a nation of heroes. It is up to you to father them. May all the warlike and generous virtues flow with the maternal milk in the hearts of the mothers of France." He then presented the women with a branch of laurel, "emblem of courage and of victory."[90]

David, the artist, Montagnard deputy and spokesperson for the Committee of Public Instruction, described the women's participation to be depicted as follows:

> One will encounter, under a portico or *Arc de Triomphe,* the heroines of 5 and 6 October, 1789, seated like they were then on their cannons; some will carry branches, others trophies, unequivocal signs of the brilliant victory that these courageous citizenesses achieved over the servile bodyguards....On the monument there will be inscriptions which will retrace these two memorable days.[91]

On one side was to be inscribed "5 and 6 October; the people, like a torrent, inundated their [the tyrants'} porticos. They disappeared."[92]

The women had initially wished to have the dedication of Marat's obelisk take place concurrently with the celebration of 10 August, but it did not occur until eight days later. On this date a deputation from the *Société* appeared at the bar of the Convention and asked that the Convention send a deputation to a ceremony in honour of Marat, meaning, of course, the erection of the obelisk, with a decree from the Convention stating that twenty four members would observe the ceremony.[93] *L'Ami du peuple* announced the order of proceedings, at the request of the *Citoyennes,* stating that the people would assemble at the usual meeting place of the *Société* (the charnal house at St. Eustache) at exactly three o'clock. The *cortège* would file past the point Saint Eustache, the Market of Pears, the streets of Ferronnerie and Saint Honoré in order to end up at the Rue Saint Niçaise at the Place de la Réunion where the ceremony would take place.[94] Once again the bathtub was resurrected and carried in the procession. Its purpose was to recall the horror of the crime and the murder of the patriot. Four women carried Marat's chair, table, writing desk, pen, and paper. The obelisk appears to have been financed through donations. The Jacobin Society on 15 August recorded that the Citizeness Léon at the head of the delegation of the *Citoyennes* requested that the Jacobins should make a contribution.[95]

After the ceremony which had occupied the time and thought of the *Citoyennes* for at least three weeks had taken place, it was time to get on with other projects. On the same day, 18 August, the women made an announcement at the Jacobin Club. At their head was Claire Lacombe who stated that the women's society wished to occupy itself with the public welfare, like the Jacobins.[96] This announcement opened what was to be the final round in the political participation of the *Citoyennes.* The foundation for this had been laid on 17 July, three days after the death of Marat, when a deputation from the society had addressed the Convention with their statement of aims of raising children like Marat (see previously) and educating them far from the institutions that had for so long "debased" the human race.[97] After this statement of objectives the women had remained silent for almost a month, concentrating mainly on honoring Marat and grieving for him. During this time the members of the *Citoyennes* were out of the mainstream of the nation's political life and they rejoined it only after the ceremony of 18 August. Previously the women had expressed their wishes to see nobles excluded from certain types of work that were essential to the livelihood of the poor, and particularly from military offices. Even earlier, on 19 May, in their common petition with the Cordeliers, they had asked for the arrest of suspects, the formation of a tribunal to deal with them, and a revolutionary army.[98] Now during the crucial weeks of July and August when the Convention was dealing with these very issues, the voice of the *Citoyennes* was silent. Just as the membership of the society was distancing itself from the government, it seems likely that the government was beginning to withdraw the pillar of support provided up until that time to the women's club.

Throughout the summer months the society maintained and even strengthened its ties with the *enragés*. Although they had severed ties with Roux in June, they were still entwined with Hébert and especially with Théophile Leclerc, another prominent member. Both Claire Lacombe and Pauline Léon were in fact romantically involved with Leclerc at different times during the life of the society. Dissensions occurred because not all members subscribed to the perspective of the *enragés*, which was fostered by Lacombe and Léon. There existed other members who were closer followers of Hébert and Robespierre and at times the emotions and beliefs of the members of the society were far from harmonious. Club members, after their declaration to the Jacobins on 18 August, began to circulate their petition outlining the basis for public well-being as they visualized it. Its reception in the popular societies was positive and on 26 August a deputation from the club presented itself at the bar of the Convention. Claire Lacombe presented the petition. She began by protesting the "prevarications without number" which had taken place, particularly in the Ministry of the Interior. She announced that the women had come to demand the implementation of the new Constitution. She complained that "we did not so vociferously demand this Constitution in order that it can be violated with impunity." It was not enough to have made the laws. It was also necessary that the people should experience some positive results. According to Lacombe, the population observed with indignation that while they

perished from misery, there existed some who "fattened themselves
on the blood of the people." She stated that the women no longer
believed in the virtue of these people who covered themselves in a
mantle of patriotism in order to indulge themselves with impunity in
"injustice and brigandage." She announced that the women knew
that the nobles had defenders within the Convention. "Deprive them
of all the places that they occupy. Do not say that this would disor-
ganize our armies by depriving them of experienced leaders; the more
talented they are, the more dangerous they are." The perfidious nobles,
she continued, should be replaced with brave soldiers who, up until
that time, had been supplanted due to intrigue. If crime had prefer-
ence under the rule of despotism, then "under the rule of Liberty,
only merit should be honoured." On the subject of the treatment of
suspects, the women's petition questioned the executive power and
its use of authority. Lacombe had this to say; "You have decreed
that male suspects will be put under arrest; but is it not a derisory
law when male suspects are the ones that are appointed to execute
it?" Was this the compensation that people would receive for the
misfortunes they had suffered for liberty? Lacombe declared the
answer to be resoundingly in the negative. The people, she stated,
would not be obliged to take justice into their own hands. Instead,
she said, the Convention should decree the "destitution" of those
administrators who were traitors to their duties, do the same for all
former nobles, and decree male conscription. Then the Convention
would have saved the country.[99]

The women of the general population had concerns other than those
of the public well-being as presented by the *Citoyennes* that day in
their petition. Throughout the summer months the capital had been

plagued with a severe shortage of bread and on 5 September the women rose in protest. Although the women of the *Citoyennes* were not without interest in the problem of subsistences, it definitely was secondary to their main political concerns during the first four months of the society's existence. A noticeable scarcity of protest with regard to shortages had emanated from the society during this time. There had been reference to it only twice before September.[100] The membership was slow to become involved in the economic aspect of problems which women were facing at this time. This was due to the society's strongly political orientation. This unmistakable political bent gives the lie to the assertion that the women's only motive for revolutionary involvement stemmed from their roles as housewives. However, the hardship of the summer of 1793 resulted in a change in attitude. Flour was scarce in the capital and women stood in long bread lines for hours, sometimes rising as early as two a.m. in the hope of being able to buy bread before the meagre supply had been depleted. At this time the members of the *Citoyennes* did become involved. Police records of that summer describe the incidents which sometimes occurred at the bakers' doors while the women waited, losing money every moment from their small wages if they were forced to remain past the time when their own work began. Often they received no bread after a long and miserable wait. The Commune attempted to deal with the problem, decreeing on 6 September that "it is forbidden of all good citizens to show up at the doors of the said bakers before six o'clock in the morning. The sections will see, each one in their (sic) arrondissement, an imposing force at the door of each baker, in order to maintain there good order, and to facilitate the distribution to good Republicans who love the laws, their magistrates, and their country."[101]   Two days later the report of the police observer Rousseville stated that as a consequence of the decree of the sixth "the people are found at the doors of the bakers between four and four-thirty in the morning and the tumult is less than usual."[102]

Equally as aggravating as the shortage of bread was the shortage of coal and of other basic necessities. The masses believed that they too were entitled to a lifestyle which at least alleviated abject misery. They felt that some legislation should be passed to ensure such a change, that it should be complement to the political terror which was being demanded and that it should outlaw hoarding and allevi- ate tax burdens on the poor. The insurrection of the first week of September was triggered by these issues. During the latter part of August the members of the *Citoyennes* served mainly as vociferous complainants on the subject of hoarding. One example of this in- volvement was the Auger case. The executive members of the *Citoyennes* persuaded the employees of Auger, a wholesaler, to re- port on the details of his business, in which he profited from the sale of food. The women of the society's executive met with their in- formants and composed a denunciation of Auger which they deliv- ered on the 21 August to the revolutionary committee of Auger's section and to the General Council.[103]

The escalating discontent of the population resulted in a major disruption in the Convention on 4 September. A deputation from the people was allowed to enter and it was followed by a huge crowd. Women were definitely present. Soon the room was full of men and women shouting "Long live the Republic!" In the crowd there were citizens carrying signs which read "War on the tyrants, war on the aristocrats, war on the hoarders." At the head of the deputation were several officers of the Commune and the mayor. The spokesman for the deputation had already delivered his message before his followers were invited to the meeting by Robespierre, the president of the Convention. Introduced by the mayor, the *procureur* of the Commune, Chaumette, presented the petition. He articulated the sources of the people's discontent, saying that a new class of tyrants had arisen, "not less cruel, not less greedy, not less insolent than the old one" and that they were "elevated on the ruins of feudalism." These people, he said, had bought the property of their ancient masters and "they continue to march in the paths made by crime, to speculate on the public misery, to exhaust the sources of abundance, and to tyrannize the destroyers or tyranny." Another class, just as greedy, just as criminal as the first, continued, he said, its robberies in the shadow of the the law. He complained that although the deputies had made wise laws that promised happiness they had never implemented them because the executive power had been weak.[104]

Chaumette then appealed for the immediate formation of a revolutionary army so that the people's request for the necessities of life would be honored and enforced by a law with teeth in it. The deputation, he stated, was requesting "peace to men of good will, war on the starvers, protection of the weak, war on the tyrants." Chaumette also described the insurrection itself stating that an immense gathering of citizens had taken place during the previous evening and early morning in front of and inside the building where the Commune met.[105] The insurrection was by no means small, once again there were definitely women present, and among those women were members of the *Citoyennes.* This day, 5 September, is often taken to mark the beginning of the Terror. It was during the Convention's debates that Billaud-Varenne advocated that terror should be the order of the day and that all dissenting elements, all enemies of the Revolution, should be tried before a revolutionary tribunal and, if found guilty, sentenced to death.[106]

THE MOUNTAIN AGAINST THE *CITOYENNES*

Although the women of the *Citoyennes* had by their actions from the spring through the insurrection of 5 September, 1793, helped bring the Mountain to power and to install the great Committee of Public Safety with its policy of terror, the organization itself would before the end of 1793 fall victim to that terror, as would several of the leading female figures of the Revolution.

The women of the society continued during the month of September to get along with the members of the Paris Jacobin Club but in many ways their relationship with the Jacobin government deteriorated in that time. On 13 September the *Citoyennes* presented their famous address to the Jacobin Club requesting the incarceration of "public women" as well as suspected "aristocrates."[107] Also on this day the minutes of the Jacobin Club record that there had been a complaint by a deputation from a fraternal society that many patriotic women wearing the national cockade were subjected to insults on a regular basis. This deputation requested a decree that would order all women to wear the cockade. The deputation which would present these demands to the Convention was asked to meet the following Sunday in the meeting room of the fraternal society.[108] This latter request focused on the other issue which had been a continuing problem for women.

Since April the wearing of the tricolour cockade was decreed by the Convention to be compulsory, but no one knew if this decree included women. The *Citoyennes* had from the beginning embraced the wearing of the tricolour. The club informed the Jacobins that their membership would wear it and sent an address to the forty-eight sections as well, inviting all citizenesses to follow this example. However, the wearing of the cockade came to symbolize affiliation with the Jacobins whose enemies began to maltreat the wearers. Several incidents were reported over the summer months which involved altercations among groups of women over the cockade. In June members of the *Citoyennes* complained that they had been beaten up for wearing it. By August the conflict had escalated considerably and by mid-September reports of beatings in the streets were common. For example, it was reported that on 14 September in the Faubourg Saint Germain women of the section resisted the passing of all those who were not wearing the cockade and they had been beaten up by the *poissardes* (market women) who had promised them the same treatment again the next day.[109]

The same day the women of the *Citoyennes* made a two-fold presentation to the General Council of the Commune. The first section contained their request that prostitutes and women suspected of being *aristocrates* be confined because their influence could be very evil. The second part consisted of a complaint that all citizenesses were not wearing the tricolour cockade.[110] During the same meeting a deputation from the *Société Fraternelle de l'Unité* complained of the insults that the cockade endured daily "on the heads of the patriot women." The deputation demanded a decree that all women wear the cockade. On 18 September an old woman was whipped and her clothes torn for not wearing the tricolour. At the same time women at Les Halles were pursued for wearing it.[111] A police report of the 20 September stated that if the cockades were not either suppressed or made mandatory for all women the results would be terrible. In some sections it was being trampled, in others, treated with more respect than ever. At the gates of Saint Denis and Saint Martin many women were reported to be wearing it. At Les Halles women were threatened if they did not.[112] In some of the markets the patriot women had been insulted by the *poissardes* who would barely tolerate the cockades and they had even been whipped for wearing them at the market at Saint Eustache.[113]

On 20 September it was reported by the police spy La Tour-la-Montagne that the women were always in a state of agitation brought on by troublemakers in order to create revolt in Paris under the veil of the cockade. He stated that up until the day before they had been whipping the women who did not wear it but that now the women who did were also threatened. "The market women at Saint Martin were armed with clubs and made the most uncivil proposals." This "war of cockades," in the spy's opinion, masked a wider and much more serious agitation which was deemed to be of a general, not partial, nature. The women were agreed, he said, on one point. This was the need for a new order of things which would release them from the misery in which they were mired. The women, this observer stated, were complaining to all the authorities, demanding the renewal of the Convention, of the administrations, and most shockingly of all, he believed that if the women "had not yet the name of the King in their mouths, it was appropriate to fear that they had it already in their hearts." A woman in the Faubourg Saint Antoine, he reported, was heard to say, "If our husbands made the Revolution, we will know how to make the counter-revolution, if it is necessary."[114]

The women continued to act out their discontent. The next day, 21 September, the spy Rousseville stated in his report that the women were gathering in large numbers at the bakers' doors and were complaining on the Rue de Sèvres that they would rather buy bread than wear the cockade.[115] The same day a delegation of members from the Paris police administration appeared at the Convention and denounced the violence perpetrated by "women who were internal enemies" against the citizenesses *patriotes* who wore the tricolour. The deputation requested punishment for those who wrenched the cockade from those honourably "decorated" with this sign of patriotism. One of the deputies converted the petition to a motion that all women should have to wear the national cockade "because where there exists divisions or fear of troubles over this civic usage, the law must intervene, and the cause must be decided in favor of patriotism." This proposition was decreed and the members of the Convention passed to the daily business, having made law the punishment of those who dared to insult the national colors.[116] But later in the day the decree was discussed at some length again in the Convention. A secretary read a summary of it and two members spoke. Deputy Mailhe asked that any woman who neglected to wear one be regarded as counter-revolutionary and suspect and that she be treated as such. The other member who spoke was the deputy from Toulouse, Jullien, who felt that the measure was "rigorous." He argued that a woman could have lost her cockade or simply forgotten to put one on. That would not be a crime. However, he emphasized that such an oversight might be carried out deliberately by a woman of royalist persuasion. It was necessary, he said, to get to this branch of counter-revolution which by its social and physical influence is able to sway opinion so effectively. He made a suggestion aimed at conciliating all interests. He suggested that the first time a woman was found to be without the cockade she would be punished with eight hours of restraint; the second time it happened she would be regarded as suspect and locked up until the peace. Jullien's proposals passed into law. With regard to Mailhe's proposal the Convention decreed that any woman who removed the cockade of another woman would be incarcerated for six years.[117] The next day a police report stated that the decree had not achieved the desired effect and troublemakers had been overheard in the Jardin de l'Egalité telling the women that they had just as much right as the men to participate in the government of their country, that they must reclaim the right to vote in the sections and be eligible for all civil and military positions. The police spy did state that in general, however, the decree was met with approbation.[118] On the same day another report stated that the decree which ordered all women to wear the cockade put an end to many small insurrections which would have become dangerous and in general the people applauded it "with enthusiasm."[119]

Despite such reports, agitation was still rife among the women. On the same day, 22 September, Rousseville reported that the women of the *Citoyennes* had met with officials of the section Croix Rouge and demanded ministerial responsibility, the organization of four revolutionary tribunals, the execution of Marie Antoinette and Brissot within a week, and the nomination of a central committee, composed of deputies from all the sections.[120] Meanwhile, the president, Claire Lacombe, was leading the group increasingly in opposition to the government and increasingly into disfavour. Known for her affililiation with the *enragés* and her outspoken support for their programs and anti-Jacobin criticisms, her problems had crystallized in a meeting of the Jacobin Club on 16 September. A secretary had announced that the society was taking the part of Théophile Leclerc, who was a friend of Jacques Roux, and that Claire Lacombe had written to the woman who had denounced Leclerc to the Committee of Public Safety and demanded that she appear and explain her conduct. One of the members of the Jacobin Club, Basire, stated that the society had also sent a delegation to the same committee requesting the release of one Semandy.[121] Semandy had been denounced and was imprisoned. The women had also tried to intervene on behalf of the mayor of Toulouse, a known aristocrat, and secure his release. At this same time, the minutes of the meeting state that a citizen began to attribute to women all the troubles that had occurred in Paris. Another member, Taschereau, stated that the Citizeness Lacombe had been busy everywhere. He said that at a meeting he attended elsewhere she had demanded "first the Constitution, all the Constitution, nothing but the Constitution" in language that was hypocritical and *feuillantin*, meaning, in general terms, anti-revolutionary. After this, he said, she wished to "undermine the basis of the Constitution and overthrow every type of constituted authority."[122] The next speaker stated that Lacombe "is strongly dangerous in that she is strongly eloquent," being in her remarks critical of the Jacobins and of the Convention. According to the minutes, Claire Lacombe appeared at that moment in the gallery and this caused a great commotion. In fact the minutes record that the tumult and the trouble became so strong that the president signalled the end of the meeting and it was only after a long time that calm was restored.[123] The report of this meeting in *Le Moniteur* is more detailed. It states that Chabot, deputy from the Cher-et-Loire, declared that Lacombe's proposals were "the most *feuillants*" in nature. She had announced that certain prisoners could not be incarcerated any longer as they must be interrogated within twenty-four hours. She had stated that it was necessary to free them if they were innocent and to send them promptly to the guillotine if they were guilty. She dared to attack Robespierre and Chabot concluded by demanding that the Jacobin Club authorize "violent measures" against the women of the *Citoyennes*. Bazire then gave details of his encounter with Claire Lacombe when she had come to the Committee of Public Safety as part of a deputation from the society and had asked to be given access to the prisons and permission to free the prisoners if she thought it appropriate. Bazire concluded by requesting that the *Citoyennes* be forced to purge their membership of all women "whose spirit has damaged the Society."[124] Ultimately it was decreed unanimously that the Jacobin Club should divest itself of all members suspected of being enemies of the nation and that it should turn them over to the Committee of General Security. An amendment was added to the effect that Claire Lacombe should be taken before the Committee immediately.[125] Once before the Committee, Lacombe was not allowed to speak. A few days later she posted a lengthy report of the incident, giving details of her humiliation. She stated that "it would be difficult to describe the effects that [my] just demand produced."

The women in the gallery rose and shouted "Down with the intriguer! Down with the new Corday!" and, by threatening to cut her to pieces, caused her to fear for her life. She was then surrounded by by a great number of members who used the same language as the women had and most of those in the galleries applauded.[126]   Subsequently, Lacombe was taken before the Committee of General Security but was released during the night.

This episode demonstrates the split that had occurred among the women of Paris and even between members of the *Citoyennes* itself. There were those who still followed Lacombe and supported her association with the *enragés*. Others adhered to the Jacobins and favored the increasing alienation of the Lacombe faction from that group. Throughout the autumn the women fought each other in the streets over issues involving lack of food and basic necessities, the wearing of the tricolour, and support or non-support of the Jacobins.   The reports of the police spies continued to describe the general unrest.

From the beginning of October the women's political thrust underwent a rapid dénouement and organized involvement unravelled at breakneck speed.   On 6 October *Le Société des hommes du 10 août* denounced the *Citoyennes* to the Convention, citing as the basis for their complaint the "unpatriotic" intentions of some women calling themselves revolutionnaries. They asked for the dissolution of the society that these women had formed.[127]   The next day, Claire Lacombe, at the head of a delegation of the *Citoyennes,* addressed the Convention. She stated that the intriguers and calumniators were not able to find the women of the Society guilty of any crimes and had dared to compare them to the Medicis, to Elizabeth of England, to Marie Antoinette, to Charlotte Corday. She declared that in the latter, nature had indeed produced a monster, but denied that the *Citoyennes* had any responsibility for or connection with the female assassin of Marat. Her next statement severely condemned the nature of men. "We are more generous than men. Our sex has produced only one monster, even though for four years we have been betrayed, assassinated by monsters without number that the masculine sex has produced." She concluded with the statement that "Our rights are those of the people and if they oppress us we will know how to resist that oppression." The *Moniteur* noted tersely that this petition was sent to the Committee of General Security.[128]   On 8 October Lacombe addressed the Jacobins and attempted to defend herself against the accusations against her. She was applauded for her efforts by the members.[129]

The same month was to witness the first paroxysm of the Terror, in which the *Citoyennes* would succumb to the policy of the Committee of Public Safety to gather all power into its own hands. The "Law of Suspects" had been adopted on 17 September, and on 10 October, the Convention declared that the government "is revolutionary until the peace," which meant that the Constitution would be set aside and provisional rule would continue through the committees of the Convention. On 13 October, the former queen, Marie Antoinette, was brought before the Revolutionary Tribunal, convicted, and guillotined on 16 October. On the last day of the month came the execution of the Girondin deputies whom the *Citoyennes* had helped to proscribe the previous June. In early November came the trial and execution of two of the most famous of the female revolutionaries, Olympe de Gouges and Madame Roland. And scarcely a week earlier the demise of the *Citoyennes* had occurred.

The events leading to the dissolution of the *Citoyennes* began on 28 October with another struggle between some of the members and the market women of Les Halles. Invited by the Réunion section to a ceremony in honour of Marat, some of the women of the society showed up wearing the red Phrygian cap, symbol of the Revolution. They were immediately attacked by the market women. The next day the minutes of the *Comité de Surveillance du Département de Paris* recorded the *rixe* or "brawl" of the previous evening between the women of Les Halles and the revolutionary women. The market women, according to this report, were protesting a plan of the revolutionary women to have it decreed that all women must wear red bonnets and pantaloons. The report of the Committee of General Security of the same day referred to the "troubles that arose in the markets as a result of the red bonnets that some women, calling themselves 'revolutionary Jacobins', wear while making other women wear them as well."[130]

The landslide which was to annihilate the women began in the Convention on the 29 October when Fabre d'Eglantine opened the tirade against them. A deputation of women had appeared in the Convention complaining that the so-called revolutionary women were trying to force them to wear the Phrygian cap. In response to their demand to dress as they pleased, d'Eglantine stated that there had already been trouble about the cockade and the Convention had decreed that the women wear it. He continued, "They demand today the red bonnet; they will not stop there. They will soon ask for a belt with pistols." He claimed that enemies of the nation were responsible for arousing the women and encouraging them to arm themselves with weapons "that they do not know how to use." As well, he complained, coalitions of women, under the name of revolutionary and fraternal institutions had been formed. The speaker declared that he had observed that these societies were not composed of ordinary women who were mothers, daughters, sisters. Rather, they were some type of female adventurers, "knights errant," emancipated women, and female grenadiers. He then requested that the Convention decree that no person could force another to dress in a manner against that individual's wishes. As well, d'Eglantine requested that the Committee of General Security "make a report on women's societies." He was applauded and a decree to this effect was passed.[131] One of the women of the group returned to the bar with the following request: "Citizens, we ask for the abolition of all the women's societies formed in clubs because it is a woman who has been the instrument of *le malheur de France* (our country's misfortune)."[132]

Two days later in the Convention, Amar, deputy from the Isère, embarked on an astonishingly brutal and fatal tirade against the *Citoyennes*. In his report from the Committee of General Security, he described the altercation which had taken place at Saint-Eustache on 28 October, when the group calling themselves "women of the Revolution" had tried to force the others to wear pantaloons and red bonnets. He reported that the fighting had become worse in the evening and some female revolutionaries were maltreated. Some, he stated, had been treated in a way that defied all decency. Undoubtedly some women had fallen victim to an excess of patriotism but others had been motivated by malice. Then Amar went in for the kill, asking two questions and giving voice to the most infamous anti-female indictment that was delivered during the Revolution. First, were women capable of exercising political rights and participating in the affairs of government? Did they possess the necessary qualities? In general, he concluded that they did not and that very few examples existed to lend support to the contrary. The political rights of the citizen, according to Amar, involve discussions and decisions relative to the interests of the state. Would women have the "moral and physical force" that the exercise of these rights would require? "Universal opinion rejects this idea." The second question posed by Amar was whether women should be allowed to hold political meetings. He described the purpose of politcal associations and concluded that women are not able to devote themselves to these questions "because they would be obliged to sacrifice to them the more important cares to which nature has called them." Amar believed that the private functions to which women are destined by nature hold as well in the general societal order and this order "results from the difference that there is between man and woman." Furthermore, each sex is called to the type of occupation which is appropriate to it. Action, he believed, was circumscribed by nature's "imperious command."

Next followed a quite amazing passage in which Amar praised the male for his greatness and superiority. "Man is strong, robust, born with great energy of audacity and courage. He can withstand perils and the intemperances of the seasons due to his constitution. He resists all the elements; he is at home with the arts, capable of difficult work." He is almost exclusively destined to agriculture, commerce, navigation, voyages, war, to everything that demands "strength, intelligence, capacity." Moreover, his nature is appropriate to profound and serious meditations which demand a great contention of spirit and long periods of study not possible for women.

Women, on the other hand, possess a quite different set of qualities. According to Amar, their purpose was to initiate the education of men, to prepare the spirits and the hearts of children for public virtue and "to direct them from happiness to well-being," elevate their souls and instruct them in the political cult of liberty. These, he stated, are women's functions, after the cares of the household! Woman is destined by nature to lead others to love virtue and when she has fulfilled these duties she will have been a credit to the *patrie*. Undoubtedly a woman must be cognizant of the principles of liberty in order to pass them on to her children, but the matter of participation is quite a different thing. "Does the modesty of a woman permit that she show herself in public and that she battle against men, to discuss in public questions on which depend the safety of the Republic?" Amar's response? "In general, women are little capable of high concepts or serious meditation" and if, in ancient times, women were kept within the family for their own good and out of deference to their "natural timidity," would citizens of the French Republic wish to have women "at the tribune, in political assemblies like men," while they abandon the basis of all the virtues of their sex and the care of their families?[133]

Furthermore, Amar proclaimed, women could be of use through discussion with their husbands, using their influence to maintain their husbands' integrity. "They are able to enlighten their husbands, communicate to them their precious reflection, the result of the tranquillity of a sedentary life." This is not all. The fortunate husband's love of country would be greatly strengthened in this way. And best of all, "the man, enlightened by familiar and peaceful discussions in the surroundings of his household, will report in society the useful ideas given to him by an honest woman." Amar then stated his belief that a woman must not leave her family in order to involve herself in the affairs of government.

There was also another way in which women's associations were dangerous, according to Amar. Because women lacked a moral education it was impossible for them to really understand the principles of liberty. Their presence in the popular societies, he believed, would give an active part in government to people "more exposed to error and to seduction." Women, according to Amar, are disposed to "an exaltation" that would be fatal in public affairs. The interests of the state would be sacrificed to all that the "vivacity of passions" can produce of disorientation and disorder. Furthermore, given over to the heat of public debates, they inculcate in their children, not love of country, but hatred and prejudice. He concluded by saying that "it is not possible that women exercise political rights." It was necessary instead to destroy these supposed popular societies of women that the aristocracy wished to establish "in order to get a hold over men and to divide the men in forcing them to take part in the these quarrels and to excite troubles." With virtually a word, Amar had expressed the belief that women belonged only in the private sphere and that the female public participation which had been taking place during this time of revolution and upheaval could only be considered an aberration of the natural order.

Only the deputy from the Marne, Charlier, dared to protest this relegation of women back to the stifling confinement of the private sphere. He said that in spite of the inconveniences that had just been cited, he did not know on what principle one could support taking away the women's right to peaceful assembly. He queried

whether the fear of some abuse, in this case influence of the aristocracy, where there was no concrete evidence to support the fear, could
warrant the destruction of the club itself. After all, he asked, what
institution could exist without inconvenience? Deputy Basire from
the Côte d'Or responded by proposing a method of justifying the
suspension of the societies. The Convention, he said, as the revolutionary government, was authorized to take any measures necessary
for the public safety. "It is, therefore, uniquely a question of knowing if the women's societies are dangerous. Experience has proven,
these last days, how much they are fatal to the public tranquillity.
That said, do not speak to me further of principles." He concluded
by requesting, in the interests of public safety, that the women's associations be outlawed, at least for the life of the Revolution.

The end of the women's clubs came immediately after this last
contribution, when the National Convention on 30 October decreed
that "Women's popular clubs and societies, under whatever name
they may exist, are forbidden."

During November the women made two attempts at having the
decree of 9 Brumaire revoked. They appeared on 5 November at the
bar of the Convention but were forced to leave due to shouts and
insults which were hurled at them.[134] Twelve days later a group of
the *Citoyennes,* wearing the red bonnet, went to a meeting of the
General Council of the Commune. The reception there was equally
unfriendly. The condemnation delivered by Chaumette echoed that
of Amar on 30 October. He stated that it was horrible, contrary to all
the laws of nature, that a woman should make herself out to be a
man. "In the name of this same nature, remain what you are and far
from envying us the perils of a stormy life, content yourselves with

making us forget, in the breasts of our families, while resting our eyes on the spectacle of our happy children, due to your care."[135] A few weeks later on 20 November, having been accused of behaving in a disruptive fashion, women were also forbidden to attend section meetings.[136]

The voices of the revolutionary women were effectively stilled for many months. They would not really be audible again until the days of misery and starvation which characterized the spring of 1795, when the women were pushed beyond the boundaries of human endurance and once again rose together in protest.

CHAPTER FOUR

THE YEAR III

Le pain nous manque; nous sommes à la veille de regretter tous les sacrifices que nous avons fait pour la Révolution. (We lack bread; we are on the verge of regretting all the sacrifices that we have made for the Revolution.) *Women's petition quoted in theMoniteur 23:717*

Le pain est le base de leur insurrection physiquement parlant, mais la Constitution est l'âme. (Physically speaking, bread is the basis of their complaint, but the Constitution is the soul.) Police spy Heroux quoted in Aulard's *La Réaction thermidorienne 1:741*

INTRODUCTION

The proscription of the women's political clubs at the end of October, 1793 was followed by mass executions. Women's heads fell under the blade along with those of the men and in Paris and throughout France the policy of the Terror had been implemented on a broad scale by the Committees of Public Safety and General Security, basing themselves on the authority of the National Convention. Although organized activity was forbidden, there is evidence that individual women continued to be involved in political action throughout the Year II, and that many women fell victim to the Terror. According to the old but still authoritative statistical study of Donald Greer, well over a thousand women went under the guillotine after conviction. Of those, 897 were commoners from the former Third Estate, including 137 from the upper middle class, 90 from the lower middle class, 389 from the working class, and 281 were peasants. And "of the 200 socially unidentifiable victims, ... 65 or 33% were women, though women constitute only 9% (1332) of the total

(14,080)." Greer observed also that "the incidence of the Terror was more severe for women of the privileged orders than for those of the Third Estate." There were 226 noble women or 20% of the order who were executed, and 126 nuns constituting 14% of the victims from the order of the clergy.[1]

Although it appeared on the surface that women were relatively passive during this time, evidence points to an ongoing clandestine political activity. Records show that in Paris at least one hundred ninety-five *"jacobines"* or *"militantes"* were active, or more precisely, were later accused of having been politically active during the Years II and III.[2] For example, the wife of a wine merchant, François, was referred to as a *"jacobine outrée"* (jacobin extremist) and was arrested for welcoming *"exagérés"* (also extremists) to her home. The woman Claudel, meanwhile, was arrested for participation in *"conciliabules"* or clandestine meetings at the home of François and his wife. These meetings took place in the evenings between the hours of six or seven o'clock and ten o'clock every three or four days over a period of four months. Likewise was the arrest of Anne Richard, wife of one Bodson, who was denounced for participation in these meetings.[3] In February, 1794 the *"militante"* Auxerre was denounced for saying that "they [the people] were sovereign, that the municipal officers and the authorities were only their agents." The woman Milet was denounced in April of 1794 for "Hébertist proposals," and Marie Gaillol, wife of one Dubois, was arrested in July of 1794 "for having caused trouble in the general assembly on the night of the 9-10."[4] After the fall of the Robespierrists in Thermidor, the new government faced acute economic problems paralleled by an increasingly hostile population. The months following

The Knitters. P.E. LeSueur. Courtesy Musée Carnavalet.

the repeal of the Maximum in December, 1794 saw Parisians plunged more deeply than ever into a struggle to survive within an economy ravaged by ever rising prices and consistently low wages. By spring the situation in the capital was appalling.

Between January and March, 1795, as the Thermidorean Reaction continued and the political situation again became fluid, Paris was experiencing famine conditions. The women of the people were accosted in the streets by *muscadins,* young men of the bourgeoisie, and whipped, beaten, and generally humiliated. This *jeunesse dorée* or "gilded youth" treated the women with a brutality which may have originated in political disagreement but which often manifested itself with distinctly violent sexual overtones. The streets were no longer safe for women and incidents of harassment were reported daily by the police observers. One such incident involved a mother and daughter who were accosted upon leaving the galleries of the Convention. While the mother was beaten by the group, the daughter was sexually assaulted.[5]

Meanwhile, female clandestine political activity continued and many women attended meetings, sometimes in conjunction with the men and sometimes separately, where political discontent formed the basis for discussion. Although the meetings often originated with the purpose of helping the families of imprisoned *sans-culottes,* they soon became a hotbed of insurrectional plotting and a place where the Convention was constantly criticized for ignoring its role of furthering the "well-being of the people."[6] Probably the best documented of these groups was the one which began meeting in mid-January in the faubourg Saint-Antoine and which has become known as the *"conspiration Lagrelet,"* named after one of the participants.

Seven women were among the eighteen members denounced on March 30. The conspirators were found to have a supply of arms including forty-nine rounds of bullets and about thirty rounds of powder as well as two guns, two swords, and two pistols. A woman was said to have alerted one of her relatives to the fact the "during the night of the twenty-ninth or thirtieth some of the Convention will have their throats cut and boutiques and stores will be pillaged."[7] The group reportedly had the intention of "sending delegations to the section assemblies and to the constituted authorities." It was reported that the conspirators had been surrounded and put in prison where they would have time to reflect on the maxim which states that "Society can only sustain in its breast those who abide by the laws which emanate from its will."[8]   Later, six women were put on trial for this conspiracy along with nineteen men.[9] Although overt organized political participation may have ended after October, 1793, this kind of evidence serves to illustrate that the women were still active, albeit in a manner much more secretive than previously.

The harsh conditions of the winter months of 1795 brought increasing hardship to a population already struggling to survive. While a small but wealthy segment of the population enjoyed a life of luxury, the majority experienced a "deep feeling of sadness." If the present seemed terrible the people "feared even more for the future."[10] Temperatures were extremely cold for Paris with readings sometimes plunging to ten degrees below freezing and on 4 Pluviose (23 January, 1795) the thermometer registered 16 degrees below freezing, one of the lowest readings in Paris during the eighteenth century.[11] The days of mere scarcity were over. The Seine was frozen and boats could no longer be used to provision the city. The bread ration dropped ever lower and hunger combined with the intolerable cold to bring about many deaths. Many others were the result of suicide. One police report of late December stated that " a woman had been found lying in her room, stiff from cold; all possible means were employed to try to resuscitate her."[12]   Later on there were many such reports per day. As the misery of the people increased, unrest in the capital once again became the main topic of the police reports.

In mid-March the women began to congregate and to formulate petitions of complaint, such as the one from the faubourgs Saint-Jacques and Saint-Marcel addressed to the Convention. This one read, "We lack bread. We are on the verge of regretting all the sacrifices that we have made for the Revolution."[13]   Two days later in the section of the Republic, the women threatened once again to march on the Convention. Women were everywhere in the demonstrations during those unhappy days, but at the hour of the distribution of bread and meat each one would disappear from that front as she went to try to obtain food for a family that had already suffered enormously and for which she was responsible.[14]   Many brochures were posted around the city at this time which appealed to the people to rise up and demand the application of the Constitution of 1793. These appeals targeted not just the *sans-culotte* but his wife as well. Some in fact were written by women. A case in point was the pamphlet entitled *Le Réveil Républicain par une démocrate* and was written by the Citizeness Dubois. In it she complained of the scarcity of bread and other basic necessities and of the increasing wealth of the merchants. She argued that the rights of the people had been confiscated, that the Convention must be concerned with the well-being of the nation or it would have betrayed its oath to the people, and she proclaimed that the people must rise up and insist upon the Constitution.[15]

The story of Grande Nanette, a laundress from the Section St. Marcel, who took action on 15 March against the Convention, is one example of a woman who could have been acting in response to these various calls to arms. Nanette and others like her joined a delegation headed for the Convention and caused a disturbance upon departure. She insulted the commissaires and made derogatory comments about the Convention and proclaimed that "the Section Starve-to-Death is going to demand bread from these beggars and reprobates. It is necessary to deal with them firmly." Nanette's group demanded that the deputation not flatter the Convention, but simply insist upon bread. Once arrived at the Convention, Nanette and one of her comrades entered in the wake of the delegation to make sure that the delegates did not grovel in front of the deputies.[16]

On 23 March the female workers at the Arsenal threatened to throw into the river the *muscadins* who came to the faubourg Saint-Antoine to intimidate the workers.[17] Police reported on the same day that a woman "who had trampled the cockade under her feet" had been arrested.[18] The next day four of the most heavily populated sections of Paris, including Marchés and Lombards, received no bread at all. On 27 March the police reported that at the door of a baker's shop in the section Observatoire, "women wrenched the cockades from other women, threw them into the air, and trampled them underfoot, all the while making indecent proposals against the Convention and the Republic."[19] Many other incidents of a similar nature occurred during these last days of March and the women were accused of attempting to instigate riots. On the twenty-first of the month (1 Germinal of the Year III), a group of women went in the company of men of the faubourg Saint-Antoine to complain to the Convention about the shortage of bread. The police spies remarked at this time that in the group there were many women, *instigatrices,* provoking the citizens to revolt.[20] The same day a woman disrupted the debate in the Convention by shouting that the royalists were assassinating the patriots.[21] Bread was obviously not the only issue brought to the fore during these days of misery.

GERMINAL

On 26 March (7 Germinal) the women tried to incite the men to march on the Convention. It was reported by police spies that women in the rue Martin "made seditious proposals and they said among other things that the men were cowards and did not show themselves and that it was impossible to live with such bad bread and so little of it." As well, the women from one of the flour shops went to the other workshops in order to force the women who were there to join them in going to the Convention.[22] Processions and protests got out of hand and arrests were made. On 27 March (8 Germinal) women from the section of Gravilliers marched on the Convention and the debate that preceded their entry illustrates the fear that the women had inspired in some of the deputies. One of them, Sautereau, of the Nièvre, stated that he had just heard the women shout "Down with the Convention!" He said that the women's intention was not so much to obtain bread which perhaps they were not even lacking, but rather to express royalist loyalties. "These shouts," he said, "are not those of republicans, but of royalists." He then asked that members of the Committee of General Security, who must have information about this gathering, be present to inform the deputies. This was decreed. Another deputy, Guyomar of the Côte du Nord, requested that the citizenesses be admitted to the bar only "in the number allowed by law." This proposal also was adopted. The women, however, insisted on being admitted "en masse." Another deputy, Blad, from Finistère, insisted that the Convention keep to its decree, and if the petitioners did not wish to submit, they would not be allowed to enter at all. This also was decreed and twenty women were allowed to enter, one of whom spoke for the group, complaining that instead of the promised pound of bread, they had been able to obtain only half a pound that morning. No one wanted it. Furthermore, the citizenesses stated that it was not possible, on forty *sous* per day, to buy the food necessary to make up for the absence of meat.[23]

In response the women received from the president a speech on patriotism and glory which emphatically blamed the previous government for all the problems besetting this one. "However," the president insisted, "since the ninth of Thermidor the fortune of the Republic has changed; justice has been put on the agenda; already many evils have been repaired." He went on to say that in order to repair everything, the Convention needed calm and the virtue of the people and that the Convention shared the hardship of the people and it would use its power to help them. He then warned the women to stay clear of "perfidious insinuations" because such indulgences would hinder the arrival of supplies. Wishing neither to be duped nor sidetracked, the women responded with their usual shout of "Bread! Bread!" A long harangue from the deputy Boissy d'Anglas of the Ardèche was interrupted twice by the women. Boissy was attempting to convince the women that they should return to their section because the bread had arrived there just before they had departed for the Convention. The women retorted in no uncertain terms that they came from *all* the sections.[24]

Another part of the demonstration took place the same day and involved about six hundred women, along with a few men, who attempted to organize a meeting in the Gravilliers section. The women combed the area and forced about four hundred individuals to the door of the general assembly hall, named a president and two secretaries, and read the section of the Constitution which said "When there is oppression, insurrection is the most sacred duty."[25] The deputy Ysabeau of Indre et Loire, who described the situation to the Convention on the day the event occurred, suggested that since this crowd had refused to disband and was at that very moment marching on the Convention, the Committee of General Security had decided to act firmly and, having exhausted all means of persuasion and prudence, to do what duty required.[26] At this point Ysabeau warned the Convention that other sections were involved and a great insurrection had been planned. The women would be at the forefront of the insurrection and the Constitution was to be a major issue. Another deputy, Perrin, representing the Vosges, stated that these were not dangerous demonstrations and that the groups coming to the Convention were composed of some men, women, and children, who were carrying the Constitution.[27] In carrying the Constitution with them the women felt that they were acting within a framework of legality, their actions being justified by the Constitution. Members of the Convention saw it differently. Ysabeau claimed that most of the people in the crowd had been drinking excessively and the Constitution was being toted along just to ensure that the march was not interrupted.[28]   Under instructions from the Committee of General Security and the military the insurrection was quelled in the sections by the armed guard and by the police who ordered section assemblies to disband under threat of deportation.

The unrest continued over the next few days and the police and guard were kept busy attempting to keep the peace. The misery of the starving people continued to dominate the police reports and the journals with accounts of the ever worsening situation. For example, on 29 March a mother murdered two of her three children rather than see them die of hunger.[29]

On 1 April (12 Germinal), when the daily quota of bread was one *quarteron* or 122.25 grams maximum per person, and some sections had no bread at all, a major demonstration took place. In the section of la Cité, at nine in the morning, groups of women gathered. Led by two young drummers, they went to the Cathedral of Notre Dame (Temple of Reason) for a general, if illegal, meeting and from there they proceeded to the Convention. In the neighbouring sections of Pont-Neuf and Fraternité the women joined the action. They obtained a drum and attempted to force the Commissaires to join them in their march. In the sections of the north the men entered houses in order to conscript demonstrators while the women engaged in *taxation populaire*, fixing the price of flour and potatoes at a figure that they deemed reasonable.[30]   Finally, the crowd arrived at the Convention and it is generally agreed that among the protestors women were more numerous than men. Deputations from several sections spoke to the Convention and ensuing discussions were constantly interrupted by a chorus of women's voices. After a deputation from the section of Fraternité had complained about the inequality in the distribution of flour, the president suggested that the sooner the Convention could get on with its work, the sooner it could deal with the needs of the people. The response to this was swift and loud with admonitions to the deputies to occupy themselves with this immediately as there was no bread.[31] The president attempted to calm the crowd by praising the "devotion and strength" of the good citizens of Paris and the women responded with the familiar cry of "Bread! Bread!" When asked directly to leave the meeting hall the women's response was the same.[32] Obviously, the women were concerned about the scarcity of food and basic necessities which plagued the capital but their political discontent had once again contributed to bringing them into the spotlight in the Convention. The telling response of one of them, when the delegation was asked to leave the meeting, was "We belong here."[33]

The group from the Halle aux Blés contained a large female element. This deputation delivered an impassioned plea for reform, explaining that the Constitution was "national property" because it was sanctioned by the people. Only the people had the right to destroy it because it belonged only to them. It was necessary that the people put on it the seal of their sovereignty. The spokesperson explained that "a good government wipes out the odious regime of Terror." The complaint of the delegation was also that government had become too centralized, taking all power into its hands. The "monstrous"result of this was dictatorship. It was necessary to distribute power among various sectors, giving agriculture and commerce their due and the people of France "their tranquillity."[34] Once these things had been achieved, according to the petitioners, it would be time to convoke a legislature. The spokesperson then implored the deputies to put aside their hatred and get on with the business of governing the country. "In the name of the people, in the name of the evils that we have suffered, in the name of the widows, the orphans, and of all the victims of the last tyranny, in the name of the assassinated patriots, we beg you to give up, or at least to suspend, your hatreds." As well, he expressed the wish that a minority cease to confuse licence with liberty of opinion. Another request dealt with a request for release of deputies detained during Thermidor. To enthusiastic applause the spokesperson concluded, "A government without responsibility is not a government."[35]

Bourdon, deputy from l'Oise, proposed that the citizens of Paris be assured that the Convention would keep its promises and apply itself to the question of subsistences and the means to expedite the delivery of the rations to the hungry. This proposal was adopted and the crowd left the Convention little by little after it was stated that the Convention would occupy itself with the needs of the people. Legendre, a member of the committee which dealt with weights and measures, asked that the good citizens leave the deputies to their deliberations. "We will suspend our hatreds and our divisions and occupy ourselves solely with the good of the people."[36] The members of the Convention then used the occasion to arrest the leaders of the opposition in order that the day "be complete."[37] Three such members were ordered deported and eight more former Jacobins were arrested.[38] Between eleven and eleven-thirty p.m. the Convention declared Paris to be in a state of siege and under the military rule of General Pichegru. The insurrection had failed. The insurgents had made no significant gains and despite the promises made that day in the Convention, the situation continued to deteriorate. One month later, in sections where scarcity and attendant suffering were most severe, it was possible to obtain only two ounces or sixty grams of bread as the daily ration. By mid-May this was the situation in all the sections of Paris. On 14 May, in the rue Tixanderie, the quantity was one ounce per person per day. Even with these restrictions there was not enough bread to go around and large numbers of people each day were deprived of adequate food. The people's suffering reached levels beyond human endurance. Atrocities became daily occurrences and often mothers killed their children to end their misery. Many bodies floated in the Seine. The report of the police of the 14 May (25 Floréal) stated that the people did not seem unduly agitated given that the state of affairs had not improved. The quality of bread was no better than the previous day, there was no more of it, there still existed the inequality of distribution, the prices of necessities of all kinds were increasing hourly at an unthinkable rate, and hoarding was an ongoing problem. Yet the people seemed to be relatively calm. Believing, however, that their report should be accurate, its authors went on to describe the actual condition of the people. In fact, they asked, in this time of great difficulty where so many citizens were dying from deprivation and when "desolate mothers, wailing at the loss of their children that they can no longer help, are suffering," in a time when suicide had never been so common, should this prevailing calm not be regarded as "the calm of death?" Was it not possible to interpret this apparent tranquillity as mere hopelessness? The people no longer had the energy to battle the scourges which had united to paralyse society.[39]

The next day *La Gazette Française* reported that "the number of suicides is truly horrifying in this unfortunate municipality. Scarcely a day passes that some men or women do not, due to despair, throw themselves into the river."[40] Earlier, between April ninth and twentieth, at least seventeen persons were retrieved from the water. On 14 May (25 Floréal) it was reported that a woman was heard to tell her child that "It was here on the tenth of August that your father's blood was spilled....I will smash your head on this same pavement rather than see you die of hunger."[41] In all parts of the city, it was reported, "One heard only complaining and wailing; one wished every moment for death and the end of a life that was no longer tolerable."[42] The report on 29 Floréal stated that "the women especially appear very discontent with the scarcity of necessities, the small amount and poor quality of bread that they receive, the slowness of its arrival." They were beginning, it was reported, to doubt the announcements of an approaching abundance. On 20 May (1 Prairial) the report read as follows: "There are always murmurings on the part of the people at the doors of the bakers. The wrath spreads in invectives and more seditious proposals against the constituted authorities; the women especially, being much less patient, seem to be much more agitated." This report also stated that the women provoked the citizens to disorder and "encouraged them not to take the small portion of bread allotted them."[43] In fact, the stronger among them, in refusing their pitiful ration, often turned their wrath upon their weaker sisters, threatening to whip them or pull them by the hair if they tried to take the portion of bread that the others had refused.[44]

Throughout the spring of 1795 the *Agence des subsistances* (welfare agency) was constantly besieged by angry women complaining of the problems encountered in their attempts to feed their families. The women often took the commissioners with them to the Convention as spokespersons but more often than not they appeared more like hostages. The women had good reason to hate the authorities for being unfair in the distribution of food, for laughing at them in their impoverished and starved condition, for their lack of sympathy and for their disrespectful, and sometimes obscene, remarks. The commissioners were known to have suggested that the women could eat hay, boards, or even "wipe their *derrières* and lick their fingers."[45] In return, the women used bad language and made obscene gestures. The relationship between the two groups was not ideal.

By 18 May the women were increasingly showing signs of severe agitation and readiness to take the law into their own hands. "The women shouted obscenities against the Convention in saying that the men had endured the hunger with the same "laziness" that they had let innocents be guillotined before their eyes.[46] From *Le Messager du Soir* of 1 Prairial came the news that the day before in the rue Arcis, some women who were at a wine merchant's saw a wagon of bread. The women left their glasses and bottles and threw themselves with energy on the wagon, taking several loaves of bread for which they paid a price determined by *taxation populaire*. The women were chased from their first refuge by a "brave patriot" and they ended up in a neighbouring pastry shop where they were allowed to use the scales in order that "they could put more equity and justice into their activities." They were reported to have stated that since the Convention had stolen their *assignats* (revolutionary bonds) when it needed them, they now had the right to take their neighbour's bread when dying of hunger. Each one of the women repeated the phrase, *"Nécessité contraint la loi"* (necessity determines the law).[47]

The expressions of discontent increased steadily. "Violent mur-murs excited by feelings of need" were accompanied by insults and threats directed at the deputies. It was most often the women, "pressed by hunger and by the cries of their children," who complained the most vociferously.[48] The women's voices, joining with those of the men, were said to form "a lamentable concert" and presented, at the same time, a very sad spectacle. The theme everywhere was "What will become of us? How will we get the harvest in? Not only are we reduced at present to the smallest portion of what is necessary to survive, but the bread is barely edible."[49] To make matters worse, the price of basic necessities was increasing hourly. The poor were forced to sell their furniture in order to subsist and often were driven to criminal activity in order to stay alive.

PRAIRIAL

On 20 May (1 Prairial) the people of Paris rebelled against the inhuman suffering which had become their lot. Early in the morning they began gathering in the various sections planning to march once more on the Convention. The women were instrumental in what was about to take place. A brochure entitled *Insurrection du peuple, pour obtenir du pain et reconquérir ses droits* (Insurrection of the People for the Purpose of Obtaining Bread and Regaining Rights) had been circulating in the city since the previous day and it contained a plan for the uprising. The plan was communicated to the deputies if the Convention on the morning of 1 Prairial by a member of the Com-mittee of General Security. It stated, among other things, that the government was starving, incarcerating, and killing the people, that such a government could only survive due to the people's weakness, and that under such circumstances, "when oppression is insufferable, insurrection is the most sacred of duties and an obligation of the first necessity."[50]

In many sections of the city the familiar drumbeat sounded early in the morning and signalled the beginning of the insurrection. As soon as they had gathered in sufficient numbers, the women headed for the offices of the civil committees of the various sections in order to commandeer the commissioners for the demonstration that would take place at the Convention. As usual the women's animosity toward the commissioners determined their treatment of them. One woman was heard to shout "Old buggar, you have a full stomach. That is why you do not wish to march with the others but you will march." Another proclaimed, "Reprobate, you have not got a long time to rule and you are actually nothing and tomorrow you will be nothing at all!"[51] Actions followed on threats and the women maltreated any individuals who seemed to be getting in their way. A group from the section of Arcis, having beaten up an adjutant at the Pont au Change and stolen his drum cases, then proceeded to wrench the épaulettes from the uniform of a policeman and cut them into tiny pieces.[52] The general mood was one of hostility. Many of the citizens of the city were reported to have arrived in the morning in a hostile mood. They were heard to threaten those whom they regarded as enemies. Many had "Bread and the Constitution of 1793" written on their hats.[53] The women forced many in their paths to go with them. In several sections they entered boutiques and ateliers and conscripted workers to join them. Once again, it seems that they were most severe with other women, holding them by their skirts, throwing stones at them, and generally threatening them with dire punishments if they did not support the march.[54] The crowds that made their way from the sections to the Convention were large and unruly. This immense crowd was animated mainly by a sense of despair. "Fooled so many times by beautiful promises that produced nothing, the citizens, embittered by hunger and misery, aroused themselves *en masse* today to go to the Convention and demand bread," reported *Le Messager du Soir* on the 2 Prairial. The women were without question in the forefront of the insurrection. They were heard to proclaim, "It is necessary that the women of the faubourgs march in front, that they traverse the streets of the merchants, bring with them all the women from the boutiques; the men will follow behind."[55] The faubourgs were in a state of "grand agitation," the like of which had not been seen since 1789, with the women prepared and ready for action. The women of Les Halles were expecting momentarily to be taken to the Tuileries. Guards were performing frequent patrols in the section Palais-National. The women at the doors of the bakers' shops "exploded in insults and threats against the national representation."[56]

This was without a doubt primarily a women's insurrection. It is certain as well that it was an insurrection of a most serious nature. "Never has a parallel thing been seen in the existence of this grand city. Neither the fourteenth of July, nor the tenth of August, nor the thirty-first of May has seen military dispositions as extraordinary."[57] The women's forceful political statement could not be ignored and they were determined to be recognized. They were in the process of demanding the right to be acknowledged and to speak, to be listened to, and to receive a response. It was reported that most of them were saying, "It is necessary that all of Paris rise and march on the Convention; we must not leave until they have given us bread; for too long a time they have put us off us to the next day."[58] They were also reported to have said once again that "the men will follow behind."[59]

When the Convention began its sitting at eleven a.m. many women were already in the galleries. The large crowd of demonstrators was also converging on the Tuileries. The behaviour of the women already there greatly annoyed the deputies. When a proclamation to the citizens of Paris was read, containing many flowery phrases to the effect that the members of the Convention understood the suffering of Parisians, the women's anger erupted into catcalls and derisive shouts. It was reported that the women were filling the last gallery and they climbed on the benches and shouted for bread. The president threatened to adjourn the meeting if the women did not calm down. The women refused to listen. Some were laughing at the turmoil. Others shook their fists at the president and the deputies. Women in another gallery on the other side joined in the shouting, also demanding bread. The deputies sat there "with the greatest calm." After about fifteen minutes the tumult ceased, but still the women would not allow the deputies to speak without interruption.[60]

In attempting to restore order, the president stated that "These terrible cries announce to us that the storm is about to break." He then attempted once more to reassure the women, telling them that the bread that they were asking for was the subject of the deputies' greatest care. "We occupy ourselves day and night with procuring it for our fellow citizens." In response, the cry once again went up from the women, "Bread! Bread!" Again the president threatened to adjourn the meeting. It took another quarter hour for the women to calm down. The president warned that all this shouting would not hasten the arrival of bread "by even an instant," a comment to which one of the women responded, "We have waited long enough, fucker." The great majority of the deputies rose and demanded that the woman be arrested. Another woman, seated next to this one, rose and shook her fist at the president. One of the deputies demanded that the president empty that gallery and he indicated the one to the left. This caused another outbreak of noise and threats from the women. The president made another attempt to calm the women, reassuring them that the situation would soon improve, but more than once he was interrupted by the women's shouts, "No! No! We want bread!" One of the deputies asked, "Would the Convention be afraid?" Another, Féraud, who was in charge of provisioning the city, added, "Let us know how to die, if it is necessary." The women then shouted and threatened him particularly.[61]

Dumont now took the presidential chair from de Vernier and immediately proclaimed that he would sooner die than be disrespectful to the Convention. While all the members rose as a sign of support, the women laughed and shouted. The women, in fact, made so much noise that it was impossible to hear the next speaker, Louvet. The President then issued another warning. "For the last time, I am declaring to the tribunes that I will give the order to have them evacuated, to arrest the agitators, and to turn them over to the tribunals." The deputies applauded while the women responded with "violent mutterings." An officer of the army went over and spoke to them authoritatively but with little result.[62]

Boissy, deputy from the Ardèche, now took over the President's chair. Louvet resumed his interrupted speech with demands that the women be punished for their behaviour. He stated that it was not possible that all the good citizens observing the meeting did not constitute the majority and it was also impossible that they were not gathered there to put a stop to the seditious shouts that were disturbing the meeting. He went on to state that the deputies were there as the representatives of twenty-five million people and that fifty seditious ones would not be making the law. He said that the Convention must know how to deploy all its power because "an outrage has been perpetrated on the national representation." He then indicated the tribune from which seditious remarks had emanated and asked that the Convention arrest the guilty, proclaiming that outside the Convention royalism and terrorism reigned. At this the women shouted, "Down! Bread! Bread!" and once again it took a quarter hour before order could be restored and the women finally stopped their shouts and threats. The president called a brigadier-general to his side before he spoke again, expressing his displeasure. The women shouted for bread after his every comment. When he called the meeting back to order, the women shouted once again for bread. He asked if it would be necessary to evacuate the benches. The response of the women was the same as before. "For lack of obedience, must I arrest all those who compose [the gallery]?" At this point the deputies rose together and shouted agreement. The women simply continued to shout for bread.[63]

The large gallery to the right of the hall and the adjoining one were full of women who continued to shout and threaten. They signalled to other women who were as yet still only in the corridors to come and join them. United, they shouted for bread and the Constitution of 1793. Some shouted for the Constitution of 1789. The deputies were indignant and so were the male observers in the galleries and they spoke with *la plus ardente colère* (extreme anger) against the women. Prolonged arguments resulted. Dumont returned and explained that he had left the chair to arrange the evacuation of the galleries. He read his proposal to that end and it was immediately adopted. The president began to order the evacuation which was to be executed with armed force and the women responded by shouting that they would not go, but one group of women exited almost immediately thereafter when violent blows were heard on the door to the left of the President's chair. The President charged a brigadier-general who was near the bar with the safety of the Convention and one of the deputies, Thibaudeau, proposed that the Convention be prepared to respond to force with force and this proposition was adopted immediately.[64]

The women were asked to leave at least twice in the next few minutes. Their refusal was firm. Dumont addressed them. "The decree rendered by the Convention orders that the gallery be evacuated. I invite the good citizens who find themselves there to cede to armed force." In response the women shouted once more for bread. The deputy Auguis of Deux Sèvres joined the fray and stated that the Convention was surrounded by several batallions "which are animated with the most patriotic zeal" and which were dedicated, according to him, to the defense of the Republic and its representatives. Dumont then resumed his tirade and proposed that the Convention get rid of the "shrews" that would like to formulate the law. He concluded with the words, "Citizens, be firm, severe, and we will see the troublemakers disappear." The women shouted their disgust and annoyance and were forcibly removed immediately afterwards by the general appointed to the job. He was assisted in his task by four soldiers and two young men armed with whips. They emptied first the large gallery at the left and proceeded on to the others from which were emanating "seditious" shouts. The total operation took about half an hour.[65]

Meanwhile, the crowd outside was beating on the door in an effort to gain admission. This group was composed of both government supporters and insurgents who had converged on the Convention at approximately the same time.[66] The deputies fled to the upper rows of the galleries and the police stayed in the lower rows in order to afford them protection from the crowd which presently burst in. Part of this group joined forces with those already acting against the women and the women were definitively "repulsed." Except, that is, for one who was still in the galleries and dared once again to "insult" the Convention and to threaten it in response to the President's announcement that "calm is reestablished; the crowd is repulsed; they have arrested one of those who was directing it." As well as the dissenting voice of the woman, who was pursued through the corridors and taken, once caught, before the Committee of General Security, other voices shouted in response to the President's statement, proclaiming such action to be illegal. Tumult ensued in response to the warlike shouts of several deputies and the deputy Auguis reported that certain individuals had spread word that in the Convention they were slitting the throats of the women present there.[67]

The deputy Féraud had chosen this moment to re-enter the Convention. Not a personal favourite of the protestors, he had already been mauled by the crowd outside and his clothes were torn. At

D'APRÈS UN CROQUIS DU TEMPS.

Les Femmes chassées à coups de fouet de poste.

The women are chased from the Convention. The Moniteur.

exactly 3:33, reported *Le Moniteur* with incredible precision, "a large crowd of women and of men armed with guns, pikes, and sabres" burst into the Convention. The usual slogan, "Bread and the Constitution of '93," was written on their hats and they were shouting the same slogan. They forced the deputies off the benches and took their seats. The others filled the floor and stopped in front of the president. An altercation ensued involving one of the hats which bore the controversial inscription and a citizen was shot and stabbed as a result. Féraud, while attempting to protect the president from the twenty guns aimed in his direction, was shot. Although details are not clear, it seems that one of the protestors had tried to stop Féraud and was stabbed by an officer. In retaliation a shot was fired and Féraud was hit. "He fell and was seized, beaten, and dragged by the hair to the corridor."[68] It was reported that the shot was fired by a young woman, Marie Françoise Carle Migelly, but evidence is inconclusive. She is thought to have later been denounced for the murder but all that was really proven in the case was that she was known to have inflicted a stab wound on his corpse.[69]

The head of Féraud was paraded around the capital for many hours while the insurgents held forth in the Convention. The crowd demanded bread, but as well they asked for the Constitution of 1793, a new commune, freedom for imprisoned patriots, the arrest of hostile deputies, the return of the Montagnards arrested in Germinal, inspections to verify subsistence laws were being followed, and renewal of sectional authorities. It is little wonder that police reports of the second Prairial concluded that the shortage of basic necessities provided only a pretext for action and that the actual cause was an agitation of a political nature in which the people expressed their discontent in demanding, along with bread, "The reestablishment of the Commune, the Constitution of 1793, freeing of the Montagnard deputies, and all members of the former revolutionary committees."[70]

The remaining Jacobin deputies were able, due to crowd support, to get some measures passed. Generally, however, the effort was disorganized and the crowd could not hold on to its temporary success. During the evening the deputies were able to muster troops from supporting sections and succeeded in having the protesters expelled. The prominence of the women at every stage of the day's events illustrates the importance of their participation.

The next day the crowd rose again. The women participated but not with the same spirit of leadership as on the previous day. This day their role was of a secondary nature. They are reported to have surrounded the Convention, but made no attempt to force their way in. They were gathered in small, menacing groups and insulted the National Guard that protected the deputies but generally did not inspire violent action as they had the day before. A formidable force had been drawn up against the insurgents under the command of General Dubois. Whereas the insurgents numbered about 20,000, close to 40,000 men stood in armed opposition to them.[71] The importance of this uprising is underscored by the fact that this was the largest display of military force to be seen in the city since 1789.[72] No shots were fired and many of the troops deserted the side of the insurgents, who failed once again to follow up their temporary advantage. Instead they listened once again to vague promises from the deputies. In the evening they returned home, ears ringing with the same messages that they had received so often in the past. On 3 Prairial the Convention sent armed forces into the Faubourg Saint-

Antoine in an unsuccessful attempt to definitively end the rebellion.
They were forced to retreat. The women of the faubourg were instrumental in an appeal to sound the general alarm and to sound the
drum, because, they said, "then the men will follow after." The women
were also involved in saving one of the insurgents, Tinel, from execution. They took him home to the faubourg and it was reported
that the women had "given life to a brother."[73]

On the fourth the citizens of the faubourg were asked to hand over
the assassins of Féraud and all the arms that might be in their possession. As the army stood ready to advance, the women once again
took to the streets to defend the faubourg against the troops of General Kilmaine who later wrote, "We were surrounded by innumer-
able armed men and by a horde of shrews a thousand times more
atrocious than the men."[74] When threatened by a lack of provisions
and attack from the National Guard, the citizens split into two groups.
One was of the opinion that they should surrender. The other, and
this group included the women, wished to hold out until the bitter
end. It was reported that they inspired the men to maintain resistance.[75] Testimony given later showed that the women were armed
and active. Louise Catherine Vignot was asked if she were not among
the women who encouraged the others to block the troops from leaving the area. She was questioned about why she was in the streets
with a sword in her possession. Another woman by the name of
Ladroite was accused along with her daughter of having spent the
day making "the most incendiary and provocative proposals."[76]
Police reported that there had been groups in all sections of Paris
who had been very numerous and very tumultuous up until seven
o'clock in the evening. The women, like *furies*, were agitating the

men and shouting, "It is necessary to support our brothers of the faubourg Antoine, to stand up to the deputies, and to not give any quarter to the merchants and the *muscadins.*" [77] Reports of the police on the situation at 5:30 p.m. stated that the citizens were at this time determined to hold out against the forces sent against them. Furthermore, the report stated that the women were assembled in every street and were making a great noise. The police spy, Heroux, stated that "Bread is the basis of their insurrection, physically speaking, but the Constitution is the soul."[78] Police reports from the section du Finistère stated that at about eight in the evening "the women provoked the men to aid the faubourg Saint-Antoine."[79] However more support was needed than was obtained and the faubourg surrendered later that evening. No shots were fired.

The repression of the insurgents was harsh indeed. The Commission which was set up to administer justice sat for ten weeks and tried one hundred and thirty-two persons, condemning nineteen of these to death, six of who were deputies of the Mountain. One hundred forty-eight women were arrested in the wake of the disturbance and nineteen others were interrogated but set free.[80] A police report of the 7 Prairial reported that Paris was now "in a most calm state" and that the arrest and incarceration of terrorists and other suspects took place without a hitch. Best of all, "No one objects; the men watch, the women keep quiet."[81]

The days of Prairial were without doubt "women's days." The existing records underscore the importance of their role. The sheer numerical strength of women in the events supports this. In the words of one police spy, "If it is only one bad, lost woman, why is she not alone?"[82] Subsequent references to the events also give credence to the vital role of women. Prairial is referred to as "the day the women were at the Convention" and "the day the women caused trouble [at the Convention]" or as "the day the women worked to save the Republic."[83] The authorities considered a man to be "even more dangerous if his duties put him frequently in contact with the women."[84] The objectives of these women's days were highly political. Bread, the Commune, the Constitution of '93, freeing of deputies and former committee members, were demands undeniably political in nature.[85] As well, the crowd demanded that all authority not emanating from the people would be suspended and "all government agencies who did not obey would be punished as tyrants."[86]

The police inspectors had witnessed in many sections a violent response to the Convention's efforts to reestablish order. They had seen in nearly all the sections that the proclamation made the evening of the first Prairial against the popular movements "had provoked the greatest discontent and cries of sedition and of revolt against the Convention, notably against the representatives known for their principles of justice."[87] The women were once again active and present in large numbers in an insurrection with major political objectives.

These extensive police records combine with the reports in the daily journals to provide an abundance of proof that the women's activities during Germinal and Prairial were above all a political phenomenon.[88] Charges laid against women after the spring insurrection ranged from having expressed the "greatest joy" when the rebels got the upper hand to having belonged to the Lazowski society which was said to be one of the most interested in advocating "pillage, anarchy, and terrorism."[89] Marie Duschesne was arrested and imprisoned for having "provoked the women to revolt."[90] Another woman was "not exempt of reproach" in the "stormy moments which have troubled this Commune" when the women play the part of "detonator."[91]

Between the first and eighth of Prairial the Convention passed four decrees aimed uniquely at controlling the activities of women. This in itself speaks for the importance of the role they had played and reflects the fear that their involvement had inspired in the authorities. As previously mentioned, Dumont had, on the first Prairial, requested that the women no longer be allowed in the benches of the Convention and his proposition was approved. He said, "It is necessary to ban them from political assemblies where they have no business and where they only make trouble."[92] In response the Convention decreed that "until such time as calm is reestablished in the Commune of Paris, no woman will be admitted into the galleries of the room where the Convention is meeting and in the future they will only be admitted when they are accompanied by a "citizen," meaning a male, of course, who will "present his citizen's card to the guard who will be situated at the bottom of the staircase leading to the galleries."[93] On 2 Prairial Legendre stated that "It is necessary to invite all women to retire to their homes and not to assemble in groups." He went on to explain that he did not mean those who were waiting for bread at the doors of the bakery shops but rather he was speaking of the women who were always at the door of the Palais-National. He declared that the weakness of their sex disarms men. He would rather have his throat slit, he declared, than injure a woman. Therefore, he had to ask that they be made to stay at home.[94] On 4 Prairial the Convention issued a statement that after having heard the report of the Committee of Public Safety, of General Security and of the military the deputies had concluded that some of the agitators were men in women's clothing. There were also present, they said, "lost" women, sustained by the enemies of liberty. These women, it was stated, abuse the considerations given the weakness of their sex. They run the streets, gather in groups, sit in the galleries, and disrupt the operations of the police and the military.

> Therefore, all women will retire, until it is otherwise decreed, to their respective domiciles; those who, one hour after the posting of the present decree, are found in the streets, gathered in groups of more than five, will be dispersed by armed force, and successively put under arrest until public tranquillity can be reestablished in Paris.[95]

The number and severity of these decrees issued within so short a time demonstrate the importance of the women's participation.

Although the repression was severe, Prairial marks the apogee of women's political involvement in the revolutionary struggle and illustrates the fullest flowering of their political awareness and responsibility. The extent and dedication of their involvement speaks for itself, as does their tenacity and courage in those days of uncertainty and danger. They fought in the Convention and in the streets for the right to participate in affairs of government and they demonstrated a political dedication and understanding of which few could have dreamed in the opening days of the Revolution.

CONCLUSION

I t is obvious that the role of women in the French Revolution was far more complex than previously recognized. Rather than observing from the sidelines and from safe within the confines of their homes, a good proportion of the female population of Paris indulged in a vigorous grassroots participation which exerted enormous influence on the immediate direction of events. While it is necessary to recognize that not all women were thus involved, and that there were different motivations driving various elements at various times, it is obvious that for the most part women's political awareness and understanding expanded as the Revolution progressed. They acted as citizens despite the fact that they were formally denied the rights of citizenship. Despite the repressive measures taken during the course of the Revolution to divest women of any right to political activity and to keep them firmly outside public life, women continued, until the events of Prairial, to take part in an increasingly meaningful and effective manner. Many women demonstrated a determination to participate fully in the political life of the nation as well as an unshakeable belief in their right to do so. This female involvement became, as we have seen, part of the political mainstream in the Revolution. These women, who were far from being a homogenous group of *furies,* came from a variety of backgrounds and rallied to universal issues of humanity, of which food was certainly one, and politics definitely another. They understood, or came to understand, the realities of the intersection of the two and the result was an energetic political display which involved a surprising awareness and understanding of events in the larger revolutionary context.

Their involvement, then, was not primarily about food. The issue of bread may have been the one that brought women into the main arena of the Revolution, but once they were there, political interest triumphed. For the brief period of the Revolution women went forward from the issues that supposedly consume only the female element of the population, and plunged headlong into roles of political activism that rivalled those of the men in some of the *grandes journées.* Their activities were of primary importance on at least two occasions, the October Days of 1789 and the spring days of 1795.

The actions of the women during the October Days demonstrated goals of an undeniably political nature of the October Days was demonstrated by their behaviour in the National Assembly. Obviously, food was not their only concern. Its shortage was definitely a problem of major proportions, but the women's realization of the connection between bread and politics serves to refute accusations of political ignorance. Their treatment of the clergy on 5 October in the National Assembly was most certainly a political statement and their conduct during the meeting with the king was indicative of a surprising degree of preparedness and political understanding. Evidence cited shows that at least some of these women were determined to bring the king to live in Paris and to keep watch over him there. The whole episode of the October Days gave to women a certain awareness of their own power and an accompanying belief in their ability to be successful and to initiate and effect change. They had accomplished something of importance which they had set out to do. They were, for the time being at least, "empowered," although still politically voiceless.

Later, the club movement served to politicize women further, to help them to understand the events of their world as it existed in a state of upheaval, and, in the case of Pauline Léon, Théroigne de Méricourt, and Olympe de Gouges, at least, to demand the right to meaningful participation, including that of bearing arms in the defence of the *patrie*. *La Société des Citoyennes Républicaines Révolutionnaires* was definitely political in orientation and had as its objectives the limitation of hoarding and inflation, and its members petitioned the Assembly vigorously in their attempts to achieve this goal. Its membership helped to remove the Girondins from the Assembly and was later to terrify the Jacobin leaders. Although the years of the Revolution had witnessed a definite invasion of the public sphere into the private realm of human existence, the actions of the women of the *Citoyennes* worked in exactly the opposite direction. Women left the privacy of their homes and dared to become public participants. The whole idea of a female participation of the kind demonstrated, served, as we have seen, to exacerbate the thinly veiled fear and suspicion which characterized the attitudes of the male politicians (and there were, of course, no other kind) toward the women. The men found it necessary to retaliate against the women's activity with a barrage of repressive legislation in October of 1793 in an effort to return women to the safe and supposedly revered "private sphere." By the spring of 1795 the nature of the women's involvement indicated the existence of a sizeable element of the female population that was fully politicized, if still unenfranchised, who were not afraid to participate in the political arena. It was a group of some two thousand women and children who made the last final stand against the government during Germinal and Prairial. They were removed from the Convention by males brandishing whips. Next they were forbidden to gather together in groups. What better way to silence such *mégères* and stop them from inciting others to riot?

During the October Days of 1789 and the spring days of 1795 these women of the working class moved as a powerful and informed element in events of great significance and participated alongside their male counterparts with understanding and determination in an effort to resolve issues that were in some cases gender related and in other instances universal in scope. A few notable women, such as Olympe de Gouges and Théroigne de Méricourt, made important contributions as individuals, and somewhere between the few *femmes célèbres* and the *furies* there existed a large body of increasingly aware, involved, and dedicated female political participants, exercising their rights and responsibilities as citizens, although always without the formal privileges of citizenship.[1]

The women were themselves not unaware of the significance of their participation. The editors of a contemporary journal, *Le Courrier de l'Hymen ou Journal des Dames,* wrote the following passage in February of 1791:

> Do the men no longer remember having seen us at the attack on the Bastille, on the roads to Versailles, and on the fields of the Federation? They should beware of arousing our courage! We have made them free![2]

This work attempts to recognize the importance of the role of these women and to place them in the mainstream of revolutionary activity, which is their rightful place, and in so doing, to acknowledge that they were instrumental in shaping a modern France, and with it, a modern world. It was not until the twentieth century that women were enfranchised in France and that family law was subject to remarkable changes that brought it up to the standards of

1792.   Despite the fact that the triumphs and aspirations of these women knew virtually no immediate success beyond the era of the Revolution itself, these developments in the twentieth century speak to the modernity and relevance of their ideals.

APPENDIX

DÉCLARATION DES DROITS DE LA
FEMME ET DE LA CITOYENNE,

*À décréter par l'Assemblée nationale dans ses der-
nières séances ou dans celle de la prochaine législature.*

PRÉAMBULE

Homme, es-tu capable d'être juste? C'est une femme
qui t'en fait la question; tu ne lui ôteras pas du moins ce
droit. Dis-moi? Qui t'a donné le souverain empire d'op-
primer mon sexe? ta force? tes talents? Observe le créa-
teur dans sa sagesse; parcours la nature dans toute sa
grandeur, dont tu sembles vouloir te rapprocher, et donne-
moi, si tu l'oses, l'exemple de cet empire tyrannique.

Remonte aux animaux, consulte les éléments, étudie
les végétaux, jette enfin un coup d'œil sur toutes les
modifications de la matière organisée; et rends-toi à
l'évidence quand je t'en offre les moyens; cherche, fouille
et distingue, si tu le peux, les sexes dans l'administration
de la nature. Partout tu les trouveras confondus, partout
ils coopèrent avec un ensemble harmonieux à ce chef-
d'œuvre immortel.

L'homme seul s'est fagoté un principe de cette exception. Bizarre, aveugle, boursouflé de sciences et dégénéré,
dans ce siècle de lumières et de sagacité, dans l'ignorance
la plus crasse, il veut commander en despote sur un sexe
qui a reçu toutes les facultés intellectuelles; qui prétend
jouir de la révolution, et réclamer ses droits à l'égalité,
pour ne rien dire de plus.

Les mères, les filles, les sœurs, représentantes de la Nation, demandent d'être constituées en assemblée nationale. Considérant que l'ignorance, l'oubli ou le mépris des droits de la femme, sont les seules causes des malheurs publics et de la corruption des gouvernements, ont résolu d'exposer dans une déclaration solennelle, les droits naturels, inaliénables et sacrés de la femme, afin que cette déclaration, constamment présente à tous les membres du corps social, leur rappelle sans cesse leurs droits et leurs devoirs, afin que les actes du pouvoir des femmes, et ceux du pouvoir des hommes, pouvant être à chaque instant comparés avec le but de toute institution politique, en soient plus respectés, afin que les réclamations des citoyennes, fondées désormais sur des principes simples et incontestables, tournent toujours au maintien de la constitution, des bonnes mœurs, et au bonheur de tous.

En conséquence, le sexe supérieur en beauté, comme en courage dans les souffrances maternelles, reconnaît et déclare, en présence et sous les auspices de l'Être suprême, les Droits suivants de la Femme et de la Citoyenne.

ARTICLE PREMIER

La Femme naît libre et demeure égale à l'homme en droits. Les distinctions sociales ne peuvent être fondées que sur l'utilité commune.

II

Le but de toute association politique est la conservation des droits naturels et imprescriptibles de la Femme et de l'Homme : ces droits sont la liberté, la propriété, la sûreté, et surtout la résistance à l'oppression.

III

Le principe de toute souveraineté réside essentiellement dans la Nation, qui n'est que la réunion de la Femme et de l'Homme : nul corps, nul individu, ne peut excercer d'autorité qui n'en émane expressément.

IV

La liberté et la justice consistent à rendre tout ce qui appartient à autrui; ainsi l'exercice des droits naturels de la femme n'a de bornes que la tyrannie perpétuelle que l'homme lui oppose; ces bornes doivent être réformées par les lois de la nature et de la raison.

V

Les lois de la nature et de la raison défendent toutes actions nuisibles à la société : tout ce qui n'est pas défendu par ces lois, sages et divines, ne peut être empêché, et nul ne peut être contraint à faire ce qu'elles n'ordonnent pas.

VI

La Loi doit être l'expression de la volonté générale; toutes les Citoyennes et Citoyens doivent concourir personnellement, ou par leurs représentants, à sa formation; elle doit être la même pour tous : toutes les citoyennes et tous les citoyens, étant égaux à ses yeux, doivent être également admissibles à toutes dignités, places et emplois publics, selon leurs capacités, et sans autres distinctions que celles de leurs vertus et de leurs talents.

VII

Nulle femme n'est exceptée; elle est accusée, arrêtée, et détenue dans les cas déterminés par la Loi. Les femmes obéissent comme les hommes à cette Loi rigoureuse.

VIII

La loi ne doit établir que des peines strictement et évidemment nécessaires, et nul ne peut être puni qu'en vertu d'une Loi établie et promulguée antérieurement au délit et légalement appliquée aux femmes.

IX

Toute femme étant déclarée coupable, toute rigueur est exercée par la Loi.

X

Nul ne doit être inquiété pour ses opinions mêmes fondamentales; la femme a le droit de monter sur l'échafaud; elle doit avoir également celui de monter à la Tribune, pourvu que ses manifestations ne troublent pas l'ordre public établi par la Loi.

XI

La libre communication des pensées et des opinions est un des droits les plus précieux de la femme, puisque cette liberté assure la légitimité des pères envers les enfants. Toute Citoyenne peut donc dire librement : je suis mère d'un enfant qui vous appartient, sans qu'un préjugé barbare la force à dissimuler la vérité; sauf à

répondre de l'abus de cette liberté dans les cas déterminés par la Loi.

XII

La garantie des droits de la femme et de la citoyenne
nécessite une utilité majeure; cette garantie doit être
instituée pour l'avantage de tous, et non pour l'utilité
particulière de celles à qui elle est confiée.

XIII

Pour l'entretien de la force publique, et pour les
dépenses d'administration, les contributions de la femme
et de l'homme sont égales; elle a part à toutes les corvées,
à toutes les tâches pénibles; elle doit donc avoir de même
part à la distribution des places, des emplois, des charges,
des dignités et de l'industrie.

XIV

Les Citoyennes et Citoyens ont le droit de constater
par eux-mêmes, ou par leurs représentants, la nécessité
de la contribution publique. Les Citoyennes ne peuvent
y adhérer que par l'admission d'un partage égal, non
seulement dans la fortune, mais encore dans l'administration publique, et le droit de déterminer la quotité,
l'assiette, le recouvrement et la durée de l'impôt.

XV

La masse des femmes, coalisée pour la contribution à
celle des hommes, a le droit de demander compte, à tout
agent public, de son administration.

XVI

Toute société, dans laquelle la garantie des droits n'est pas assurée, ni la séparation des pouvoirs déterminée, n'a point de constitution; la constitution est nulle, si la majorité des individus qui composent la Nation, n'a pas coopéré à sa rédaction.

XVII

Les propriétés sont à tous les sexes réunis ou séparés; elles sont pour chacun un droit inviolable et sacré; nul ne peut en être privé comme vrai patrimoine de la Nature, si ce n'est lorsque la nécessité publique, légalement constatée, l'exige évidemment, et sous la condition d'une juste et préalable indemnité.

POSTAMBULE

Femme, réveille-toi; le tocsin de la raison se fait entendre dans tout l'univers; reconnais tes droits. Le puissant empire de la Nature n'est plus environné de préjugés, de fanatisme, de superstition et de mensonges. Le flambeau de la vérité a dissipé tous les nuages de la sottise et de l'usurpation. L'homme esclave a multiplié ses forces, a eu besoin de recourir aux tiennes pour briser ses fers. Devenu libre, il est devenu injuste envers sa compagne. Ô femmes! femmes, quand cesserez-vous d'être aveugles? Quels sont les avantages que vous avez recueillis dans la révolution? Un mépris plus marqué, un dédain plus signalé. Dans les siècles de corruption vous n'avez régné que sur la faiblesse des hommes. Votre empire est détruit; que vous reste-t-il donc? La conviction des injustices de l'homme. La réclamation de votre patrimoine fondée sur les sages décrets de la Nature. Qu'auriez-vous à redouter pour une si belle entreprise? Le bon mot du Législateur des noces de Cana? Craignez-vous que nos Législateurs français, correcteurs de cette morale, longtemps accrochée aux branches de la politique, mais qui n'est plus de saison, ne vous répètent : femmes, qu'y a-t-il de commun entre vous et nous? Tout, auriez-vous à répondre. S'ils s'obstinaient, dans leur faiblesse, à mettre cette inconséquence en contradiction avec leurs principes, opposez courageusement la force de la raison aux vaines prétentions de supériorité; réunissez-vous sous les étendards de la philosophie; déployez toute l'énergie de votre caractère, et vous verrez bientôt ces orgueilleux, nos serviles adorateurs rampants à vos pieds, mais fiers de partager avec vous les trésors de l'Être Suprême. Quelles que soient les barrières que l'on vous oppose, il est en votre pouvoir de vous en affranchir; vous n'avez qu'à le vouloir.

Passons maintenant à l'effroyable tableau de ce que vous avez été dans la société; et puisqu'il est question, en ce moment, d'une éducation nationale, voyons si nos sages Législateurs penseront sainement sur l'éducation des femmes.

Les femmes ont fait plus de mal que de bien. La contrainte et la dissimulation ont été leur partage. Ce que la force leur avait ravi, la ruse leur a rendu; elles ont eu recours à toutes les ressources de leurs charmes, et le plus irréprochable ne leur résistait pas. Le poison, le fer, tout leur était soumis; elles commandaient au crime comme à la vertu. Le gouvernement français, surtout, a dépendu, pendant des siècles, de l'administration nocturne des femmes; le cabinet n'avait point de secret pour leur indiscrétion; ambassade, commandement, ministère, présidence, pontificat, cardinalat, enfin tout ce qui caractérise la sottise des hommes, profane et sacré, tout a été soumis à la cupidité et à l'ambition de ce sexe autrefois méprisable et respecté, et depuis la révolution, respectable et méprisé.

Dans cette sorte d'anthithèse, que de remarques n'ai-je point à offrir! je n'ai qu'un moment pour les faire, mais ce moment fixera l'attention de la postérité la plus reculée. Sous l'Ancien Régime, tout était vicieux, tout était coupable; mais ne pourrait-on pas apercevoir l'amélioration des choses dans la substance même des vices? Une femme n'avait besoin que d'être belle ou aimable; quand elle possédait ces deux avantages, elle voyait cent fortunes à ses pieds. Si elle n'en profitait pas, elle avait un caractère bizarre, ou une philosophie peu commune, qui la portait au mépris des richesses; alors elle n'était plus considérée que comme une mauvaise tête. La plus indécente se faisait respecter avec de l'or. Le commerce des femmes était une espèce d'industrie reçue dans la première classe, qui, désormais, n'aura plus de crédit. S'il en avait encore, la révolution serait perdue, et sous de nouveaux rapports, nous serions toujours corrompus. Cependant la raison peut-elle se dissimuler que tout autre chemin à la fortune est fermé à la femme, que l'homme achète, comme l'esclave sur les côtes d'Afrique? La différence est grande; on le sait. L'esclave commande au maître; mais si le maître lui donne la liberté sans récompense, et à un âge où l'esclave a perdu tous ses charmes, que devient cette infortunée? Le jouet du mépris; les portes mêmes de la bienfaisance lui sont fermées; elle est pauvre et vieille, dit-on; pourquoi n'a-t-elle pas su faire fortune? D'autres exemples encore plus touchants s'offrent à la raison. Une jeune personne sans expérience, séduite par un homme qu'elle aime, abandonnera ses parents pour le suivre; l'ingrat la laissera après quelques années, et plus elle aura vieilli avec lui, plus son inconstance sera inhumaine. Si elle a des enfants, il l'abandonnera de même. S'il est riche, il se croira dispensé de partager sa fortune avec ses nobles victimes. Si quelque engagement le lie à ses devoirs, il en violera la puissance en espérant tout des lois. S'il est marié, tout autre engagement perd ses droits. Quelles lois reste-t-il donc à faire pour extirper le vice jusque dans la racine? Celle du partage des fortunes entre les hommes et les femmes, et de l'administration publique. On conçoit aisément que celle qui est née d'une famille riche, gagne beaucoup avec l'égalité des partages. Mais celle qui est née d'une famille pauvre, avec du mérite et des vertus, quel est son lot? La pauvreté et l'opprobre. Si elle n'excelle pas précisément en musique ou en peinture, elle ne peut être admise à aucune fonction publique, quand elle en aurait toute la capacité. Je ne veux donner qu'un aperçu des choses, je les approfondirai dans la nouvelle édition de tous mes ouvrages politiques que je me propose de donner au public dans quelques jours, avec des notes.

Je reprends mon texte quant aux mœurs. Le mariage est le tombeau de la confiance et de l'amour. La femme mariée peut impunément donner des bâtards à son mari, et la fortune qui ne leur appartient pas. Celle qui ne l'est pas, n'a qu'un faible droit : les lois anciennes et inhumaines lui refusaient ce droit sur le nom et sur le bien de leur père, pour ses enfants, et l'on n'a pas fait de nouvelles lois sur cette matière. Si tenter de donner à mon sexe une consistance honorable et juste, est considéré dans ce moment comme un paradoxe de ma part, et comme tenter l'impossible, je laisse aux hommes à venir la gloire de traiter cette matière; mais, en attendant, on peut la préparer par l'éducation nationale, par la restauration des mœurs et par les conventions conjugales.

Forme du Contrat social de l'Homme et de la Femme

Nous *N* et *N,* mus par notre propre volonté, nous unissons pour le terme de notre vie, et pour la durée de nos penchants mutuels, aux conditions suivantes : Nous

entendons et voulons mettre nos fortunes en communauté, en nous réservant cependant le droit de les séparer
en faveur de nos enfants, et de ceux que nous pourrions
avoir d'une inclination particulière, reconnaissant
mutuellement que notre bien appartient directement à
nos enfants, de quelque lit qu'ils sortent, et que tous
indistinctement ont le droit de porter *le nom des pères
et mères* qui les ont avoués, et nous imposons de souscrire
à la loi qui punit l'abnégation de son propre sang. Nous
nous obligeons également, au cas de séparation, de faire
le partage de notre fortune, et de prélever la portion de
nos enfants indiquée par la loi; et, au cas d'union parfaite,
celui qui viendrait à mourir, se désisterait de la moitié
de ses propriétés en faveur de ses enfants; et si l'un
mourait sans enfants, le survivant hériterait de droit, à
moins que le mourant n'ait disposé de la moitié du bien
commun en faveur de qui il jugerait à propos.

Voilà à peu près la formule de l'acte conjugal dont je
propose l'exécution. À la lecture de ce bizarre écrit, je
vois s'élever contre moi les tartuffes, les bégueules, le
clergé et toute la séquelle infernale. Mais combien il
offrira aux sages de moyens moraux pour arriver à la
perfectibilité d'un gouvernement heureux! j'en vais donner en peu de mots la preuve physique. Le riche Épi-
curien sans enfants, trouve fort bon d'aller chez son
voisin pauvre augmenter sa famille. Lorsqu'il y aura une
loi qui autorisera la femme du pauvre à faire adopter
au riche ses enfants, les liens de la société seront plus
resserrés, et les mœurs plus épurées [1]. Cette loi conser-
vera peut-être le bien de la communauté, et retiendra le
désordre qui conduit tant de victimes dans les hospices
de l'opprobre, de la bassesse et de la dégénération des
principes humains, où, depuis longtemps, gémit la Nature.

---

1. Abraham eut ainsi des enfants très légitimes d'Agar, servante de sa
femme.

Que les détracteurs de la saine philosophie cessent donc de se récrier contre les mœurs primitives, ou qu'ils aillent se perdre dans la source de leurs citations.

Je voudrais encore une loi qui avantageât les veuves et les demoiselles trompées par les fausses promesses d'un homme à qui elles se seraient attachées; je voudrais, dis-je, que cette loi forçât un inconstant à tenir ses engagements, ou à une indemnité proportionnée à sa fortune. Je voudrais encore que cette loi fût rigoureuse contre les femmes, du moins pour celles qui auraient le front de recourir à une loi qu'elles auraient elles-mêmes enfreinte par leur inconduite, si la preuve en était faite. Je voudrais, en même temps, comme je l'ai exposé dans *le Bonheur primitif de l'homme,* en 1788, que les filles publiques fussent placées dans des quartiers désignés. Ce ne sont pas les femmes publiques qui contribuent le plus à la dépravation des mœurs, ce sont les femmes de la société. En restaurant les dernières, on modifie les premières. Cette chaîne d'union fraternelle offrira d'abord le désordre, mais par les suites, elle produira à la fin un ensemble parfait.

J'offre un moyen invincible pour élever l'âme des femmes : c'est de les joindre à tous les exercices de l'homme. Si l'homme s'obstine à trouver ce moyen impraticable, qu'il partage sa fortune avec la femme, non à son caprice, mais par la sagesse des lois. Le préjugé tombe, les mœurs s'épurent, et la Nature reprend tous ses droits. Ajoutez-y le mariage des prêtres, le Roi raffermi sur son trône, et le gouvernement français ne saurait plus périr.

Il était bien nécessaire que je dise quelques mots sur les troubles que cause, dit-on, le décret en faveur des hommes de couleur, dans nos îles. C'est là où la Nature frémit d'horreur; c'est là où la raison et l'humanité, n'ont pas encore touché les âmes endurcies; c'est là surtout où la division et la discorde agitent leurs habitants. Il n'est pas difficile de deviner les instigateurs de ces fermentations incendiaires : il y en a dans le sein même de l'Assemblée nationale : ils allument en Europe le feu qui doit embraser l'Amérique. Les Colons prétendent régner en despotes sur des hommes dont ils sont les pères et les frères; et méconnaissant les droits de la nature, ils en poursuivent la source jusque dans la plus petite teinte de leur sang. Ces Colons inhumains disent : notre sang circule dans leurs veines, mais nous le répandrons tout, s'il le faut, pour assouvir notre cupidité ou notre aveugle ambition. C'est dans ces lieux, les plus près de la Nature, que le père méconnaît le fils; sourd aux cris du sang, il en étouffe tous les charmes. Que peut-on espérer de la résistance qu'on lui oppose? la contraindre avec violence, c'est la rendre terrible, la laisser encore dans les fers, c'est acheminer toutes les calamités vers l'Amérique. Une main divine semble répandre partout l'apanage de l'homme, *la liberté;* la loi seule a le droit de réprimer cette liberté, si elle dégénère en licence; mais elle doit être égale pour tous, c'est elle surtout qui doit renfermer l'Assemblée nationale dans son décret, dicté par la prudence et par la justice. Puisse-t-elle agir de même pour l'état de la France, et se rendre aussi attentive sur les nouveaux abus, comme elle l'a été sur les anciens qui deviennent chaque jour plus effroyables! Mon opinion serait encore de raccommoder le pouvoir exécutif avec le pouvoir législatif, car il me semble que l'un est tout, et que l'autre n'est rien; d'où naîtra, malheureusement peut-être, la perte de l'Empire français. Je considère ces deux pouvoirs, comme l'homme et la femme qui doivent être unis, mais égaux en force et en vertu, pour faire un bon ménage.

NOTES TO INTRODUCTION

1 Jules Michelet, *Les Femmes de la Révolution,* 7th ed. (Paris: Levy Frères, 1889); E. Lairtullier, *Les Femmes célèbres de 1789 à 1795 et leur influence dans la Révolution* (Paris: Librairie Politique, 1840).

2 Léopold Lacour, *Les Origines du féminisme contemporain: Trois Femmes de la Révolution, Olympe de Gouges, Théroigne de Méricourt, Rose Lacombe* (Paris: Plon, 1900); Marc de Villiers, *Histoire des clubs de femmes et des légions d'amazones* (Paris: Plon, 1910); Adrien Lasserre, *La Participation collective des femmes à la Révolution française: les antécédents du féminisme* (Paris: Félix Alcan, 1906).

3 Jeanne Bouvier, *Les Femmes pendant la Révolution: leur action politique, sociale, économique, militaire, leur courage devant l'échafaud* (Paris: Editions Eugène Figuière, 1931).

4 Albert Soboul, *Les Sans-culottes parisiens en l'an II: Mouvement populaire et gouvernement révolutionnaire, 2 juin, 1793-9 thermidor an II* (Paris: Librairie Clavreuil, 1958); Kare Tønnessen, *La Défaite des sans-culottes: Mouvement populaire et réaction bourgeoise en l'an III* (Paris: Librairie Clavreuil, 1959); George Rudé, *The Crowd in the French Revolution* (Oxford: Clarendon Press, 1959, 1967).

5 Olwen Hufton, "Women in the French Revolution, 1789-1796," *Past and Present* 53 (1971): 90-108; Jane Abray, "Feminism in the French Revolution," *American Historical Review* 80 (1975): 43-62.; Louis Devance, "Le Féminisme pendant la Révolution française," *Annales historiques de la Révolution française* 49 (1977): 342-376; Ruth Graham, "Loaves and Liberty: Women in the French Revolution," in R. Bridenthal and C. Koonz, eds., *Becoming Visible: Women in European History* (Boston: Houghlin Mifflin, 1977), 236-254; Darline G. Levy and Harriet B. Applewhite, "Women and Political Revolution in Paris," in R. Bridenthal, C. Koonz and S. Stuard, eds., *Becoming Visible,* 2nd edition (Boston: Houghton Mifflin, 1987), 281-306; Dominique Godineau, "Masculine and Feminine Political Practice during the French Revolution, 1793-Year III," in Darline Levy and Harriet Applewhite, eds., *Women and Politics in the Age of the Democratic Revolution* (Ann Arbor: University of Michigan Press, 1990), 61-80.

6 Darline Levy, Harriet Applewhite, and Mary Johnson, trans. and eds., *Women in Revolutionary Paris 1789-1795* (Urbana: University of Illinois Press, 1979).

7 Paule Marie Duhet, *Les Femmes et la Révolution 1789-94* (Paris: Juillard, 1971).

8 Maria Cerati, *Le Club des Citoyennes Républicaines Révolutionnaires* (Paris: Editions Sociales, 1966).

9   For example, the works of Gita May, *Madame Roland and the Age of Revolution* (New York: Columbia University Press, 1970); Guy Chaussinand-Nogaret, *Madame Roland: une femme en révolution* (Paris: Editions du Seuil, 1985); Olivier Blanc, *Olympe de Gouges* (Paris: Syros, 1981); and Elizabeth Roudinesco, *Théroigne de Méricourt: une femme mélancolique sous la Révolution* (Paris: Seuil, 1989).

10   Anne Soprani, *La Révolution et les femmes de 1789 à 1796* (Paris: MA Editions, 1988); Nicole Vray, *Les Femmes dans la tourmente* (Editions Ouest France, 1988); Catherine Marand Fouquet, *La Femme au temps de la Révolution* (Paris: Stock/Pernoud, 1989); Annette Rosa, *Citoyennes: Les Femmes et la Révolution française* (Paris: Messidor, 1988).

11   Linda Kelly, *Women of the Revolution* (London: Hamish Hamilton, 1987).

12   Dominique Godineau, *Citoyennes tricoteuses: les femmes du peuple à Paris pendant la Révolution française* (Aix-en-Provence: Alinea, 1988). For an earlier unpublished attempt, see Mary Jay Durham, "The Sans-Jupons' Crusade for Liberation during the French Revolution." Ph. D. dissertation, Washington University, 1972.

13   Godineau, "Political Practice," in Levy and Applewhite, *Women and Politics,* 61-80; Levy and Applewhite, "Women, Radicalization, and the Fall of the French Monarchy," in Levy and Applewhite, *Women and Politics,* 81-107.

14   Olwen Hufton, *Women and the Limits of Citizenship in the French Revolution* (Toronto: University of Toronto Press, 1992).

15   Sara Melzer and Leslie Rabine, *Rebel Daughters: Women and the French Revolution* (New York: Oxford University Press, 1992).

16   J. F. Bosher, *The French Revolution* (New York: W. W. Norton, 1988); William Doyle, *The Oxford History of the French Revolution* (Oxford: Clarendon Press, 1989); Owen Connelly, *The French Revolution and the Napoleonic Era,* 2nd edition (Fort Worth, Texas: Holt, Rinehart and Winston, Inc., 1991).

17   Simon Schama, *Citizens: A Chronicle of the French Revolution* (Toronto: Random House, 1989).

18   François Furet and Mona Ozouf, eds., *Dictionnaire critique de la Révolution française* (Paris: Flammarion, 1988).

19   Levy, Applewhite, and Johnson, *Revolutionary Paris,* 12.

20   Alphonse Aulard, ed., *La Société des Jacobins: recueil de documents pour l'histoire du club des Jacobins de Paris,* 6 vols. (Paris: Librairie Jouast, 1889-97); A. Aulard, ed., *Paris pendant la réaction thermidorienne et sous le directoire: recueil de documents pour l'histoire de l'esprit public à Paris,* 5 vols. (Paris: Librairie Cerf, 1898-1902).

21   Alexandre Tuetey, ed., *Repertoire général des sources manuscrits de l'histoire de Paris pendant la Révolution française,* 11 vols. (Paris: Imprimerie Nouvelle, 1890-1914).

22   *Procédure criminelle au Châtelet, instruite au Châtelet de Paris, sur la dénonciation des faits arrivés à Versailles dans la journée du 6 octobre, 1789* (Paris: Chez Baudouin, 1790).

NOTES TO CHAPTER 1

1   *Cahiers de doléances des femmes en 1789 et autres textes*, Paule-Marie Duhet, ed., (Paris: Des Femmes, 1981).

2   Rudé, *The Crowd in the French Revolution*, 37, 39.

3   Ibid., 58-59. For some examples of such scenes, see Jacques Godechot, *The Taking of the Bastille: July 14th, 1789*, trans., Jean Stewart (New York: Charles Scribner's Sons, 1970), op. 224; and Annette Rosa, *Citoyennes: Les Femmes et la Révolution française* (Paris: Messidor, 1988), 70-71.

4   S. Hardy, *Mes Loisirs, ou journal d'événements tels qu'ils parviennent à ma connoissance*, vol. 8 (Paris, 1789): 478.

5   Y. Bruhat, *Les Femmes de la révolution française* (Paris, 1939), 54. Bruhat explores the popular concept of "le bon roi" or the fairytale king in relation to the march of the women to Versailles.

6   D.M.G. Sutherland, *France 1789-1815: Revolution and Counterrevolution* (London: Fontana Press, 1985), 83.

7   P.J.B. Buchez and P.C. Roux, *Histoire parlementaire de la révolution française ou journal des assemblées nationales depuis 1789 jusqu'en 1815*, vol. 2 (Paris: Librairie Paulin, 1835): 422.

8   Tuetey, *Répertoire général*, 1:90-91, nos. 869 and 866.

9   S. Hardy, *Mes Loisirs*, 8:478.

10   *Réimpression de l'ancien Moniteur*, 32 vols. (Paris: H. Plon, 1858-63), 2:20, hereafter *Moniteur*.

11   *Procédure criminelle, instruite au Châtelet de Paris, sur la denonciation des faits arrivés à Versailles dans la journée du 6 Octobre, 1789* (Paris: Chez Baudouin, 1790), witness no. 36.

12   Buchez and Roux, *Histoire parlementaire*, 3:75.

13   *Procédure criminelle*, no. 182.

14   Ibid., no. 43.

15   Ibid., no. 92

16   Jean Sylvain Bailly, *Mémoires d'un témoin de la Révolution* (Paris: Baudouin Frères, 1821), 3:84.

17   Procédure criminelle, no. 35

18   Ibid.

19   Ibid.

20   Ibid., no. 44.

21   Ibid., no. 81. Maillard's deposition in the *Moniteur* is a shortened version.

22   Ibid.

23   Ibid., nos. 35 and 44.

24   *Evénement de Paris et de Versailles*, in *Les Femmes dans la Révolution française 1789-94. 70 imprimés reproduits in-extenso, pétitions, pamphlets, affiches, documents divers*, Albert Soboul, ed., 2 vols. (Paris: Edhis, 1982),1:2.

25   Ibid.

26   *Procédure criminelle*, no. 8.

27   *Evénement*, 1:2-3.

28   *Procédure criminelle*, no. 50.

29   Bailly, *Mémoires*, 3:85, 86.

30   *Procédure criminelle*, no. 81.

31   Ibid.

32   Ibid.

33   Ibid., no. 82.

34   *Procédure criminelle*, no. 81.

35   Ibid.

36   Ibid.

37   Ibid.

38   Ibid.

39   Ibid.

40   Ibid., no. 103.

41   Ibid., *Mémoires de la Marquise de la Tour du Pin: journal d'une femme de cinquante ans (1778-1815) suivis d'extraits inédits de sa correspondance (1815-1846)*. (Paris: Mercure de France, 1989), 115.

42   *Archives parlementaires de 1787 à 1860, recueil complet des débats législatifs et politiques des Chambres française, imprimé par order du Sénat et de la Chambre des députés, Première série (1787 à 1799)*. 82 vols. (Paris: Librairie administrative de P. Dupont, 1862; Washington, D.C.: Microcard Editions, 1967); séance 5 octobre 1789.

43   M. Mounier, *Appel au tribunal de l'opinion publique, du rapport de M. Chabroud, et du décret rendu par l'Assemblée Nationale le 2 Octobre 1790, etc.*, (Genève, 1790), 130.

44   Ibid., *Procédure criminelle*, no. 81.

45   Ibid.

46   Ibid.

47   Mounier, *Appel au tribunal*, 130.

48   *Procédure criminelle*, no. 81.

49   Ibid.

50   Ibid.

51   Ibid., no. 148.

52   *Archives parlementaires*, October 5, 1789.

53   *Moniteur*, 2:12.

54   J.J. Mounier, *Exposé justificatif de la conduite de Mounier*, 68.

55   Ibid.

56   *Procédure criminelle*, no. 187.

57   Ibid., no. 183.

58   Mounier, *Appel*, 131.

59   *Procédure criminelle*, 187.

60   Ibid., no. 183.

61   Ibid., no. 187.

62   Ibid., nos. 187 and 183.

63   Ibid., no. 81.

64   Ibid., no. 83.

65   Ibid., 183.

66   Maillard claimed that the women insisted on accompanying him back to Paris in place of the two deputies assigned by the king to do this task. It should be noted that Maillard's statements were sometimes suspect. Mounier, for instance, said that he was a braggart and a liar; Mounier, *Appel*, 136.

67   Marquise de la Tour du Pin, *Mémoires*, 118.

68   Ibid., 120.

69   Louis Gottschalk and Margaret Maddox, *Lafayette in the French Revolution: Through the October Days*. (Chicago: University of Chicago Press, 1969), 368-72.

70   *Procédure criminelle*, no. 18. Simon Schama in *Citizens*, 467, mistakenly says that Miomandre de Sainte-Marie was beheaded on October 6.

71   *Procédure criminelle*, no. 90.

72   Ibid., no. 94.

73   Ibid., no. 82.

74   *Révolutions de Paris*, no. 12, October 6, 1789, 20.

75   *Journal des Révolutions de l'Europe,* 5:76, as quoted in Adrien Lasserre, *Participation collective des femmes, 175.*

76   *Révolutions de Paris*, no. 12, October 6, 1789, 22.

77   *Procédure criminelle*, no. 148.

78   Bailly, *Mémoires,* 3:118-19.

79   *Actes de la commune de Paris pendant la révolution*, ed., Sigismund Lacroix, vol. 2 (Paris: L. Cerf, 1895): 190.

80   Bailly, *Mémoires*, 3:119.

81   Madame Campan, *Mémoires sur la vie privée de Marie-Antoinette, reine de France et de Navarre suivis de souvenirs et anecdotes historiques sur les regnes de Louis XIV, de Louis XV et de Louis XVI* (Paris: Baudouin Frères, 1823), 86-87.

82   *Correspondance d'un habitant de Paris avec ses amis de Suisse, d'angleterre, sur les événements de 1789, 1790, jusq'en avril 1791* (Paris: Chez Desenne, 1791), as cited by Lasserre, *Participation collective des femmes*, 177.

83   *Correspondance de Mercy-Argenteau*, 2:271, as quoted in A. Mathiez, "Etude critique sur les journées des 5 et 6 octobre, 1789," *Revue historique* 68 (1898): 54.

84   Memoirs of Madame de Tourzel, as cited by E.L. Higgins, ed., *The French Revolution as Told by Contemporaries* (Boston: Houghton-Miffin, 1938), 131.

85   *Procédure criminelle*, nos. 62, 91, 126, 92.

86   Ibid., no. 35.

87   Ibid., no. 101.

88   Théroigne de Méricourt maintained that she was *not* on the journey; she was living at Versailles that summer.

89   *Procédure criminelle*, no. 82.

90   Ibid., no. 103.

91   Ibid., no. 102.

92   Ibid., no. 105.

93   Ibid., nos. 106, 108, 183, 187, 284, 90, 85.

94   Ibid., no. 370.

95   Ibid., no. 225.

96   Ibid., no. 243.

97   Ibid., no. 236

98   Ibid., no. 30.

99   Ibid., no. 48.

100   Ibid., no. 90.

101   Ibid., no. 81.

102   *Lettres de Madame de M.* in *Etrennes Nationales des Dames*, Nov. 3, 1789, 1.

103   Bailly, *Mémoires*, 3:84.

104   Marc De Villiers, *Les 5 et 6 Octobre 1789: Reine Audu (les légendes des journées d'octobre}* (Paris: Emile Paul Frères, 1917) 26, 27.

105   *Procédure criminelle*, nos. 343, 81, 38, 183, 139; Bailly, *Mémoires*, 3:86.

106   *Procédure criminelle*, no. 339.

107   For a discussion of the role of Orléans, see George Armstrong Kelly, *Victims, Authority, and Terror: The Parallel Deaths of d'Orléans, Custine, Bailly, and Malesherbes* (Chapel Hill, North Carolina: University of North Carolina Press, 1982), 61-68.

108   *Procédure criminelle*, nos. 79, 18, 56.

109   For a detailed treatment, see A. Mathiez, "Etude critique sur les journées des 5 et 6 octobre 1789," *Revue historique* 69 (1899): 47-48.

110   *Révolutions de Paris*, no. 12, Oct. 6, 1789, 15.

111   *Procédure criminelle*, no. 220.

112   Ibid., no. 343.

113   Ibid.

114   Ibid., nos. 183, 187. St. Priest was later denounced in the Assembly by Mirabeau for saying to François Rolin that when they had one king they had bread and today they have twelve hundred kings and they should ask them for bread. Mirabeau referred to a *phalange* or "phalanx" of women. Saint-Priest, in defending himself, asked, "and since when is one able to call a 'phalanx' the five or six women to whom I have spoken in the Oeil-de-Boeuf?" See *Moniteur*, 2:40.

115   *Ami du peuple*, no. 27, 7 octobre, 1789.

116   *Procédure criminelle*, no. 187.

117   *Les Héroines de Paris*, in Albert Soboul's *Les Femmes dans la Révolution française*, in 1:4.

NOTES TO CHAPTER 2

1 For a thorough study of the *fêtes*, see Mona Ozouf, *La Fête révolutionnaire, 1789-1799* (Paris: Gallimard, 1976). Related themes are taken up in Lynn Hunt, *Politics, Culture, and Class in the French Revolution* (Berkeley: University of California Press, 1984) and Maurice Agulhon, *Marianne au Combat: L'Imagerie et la symbolique républicaines de 1789 à 1880* (Paris: Flammarion, 1979).

2 Godineau, *Tricoteuses*, 113-15, and Marc de Villiers, *Histoire des clubs de femmes et des légions d'amazones* (Paris: Plon, 1910), Chapter 2. Few of these societies have been studied in any detail.

3 Marcellin Pellet, *Etude historique et biographique sur Théroigne de Méricourt* (Paris: Maison Quantin, 1886), 40.

4 *Révolutions de France et Brabant,* as quoted in Duhet, *Les Femmes*, 100.

5 From the *Chronique de Paris* as quoted in de Villiers, 43-44.

6 Duhet, *Les Femmes,* 101

7 *Babillard*, no. 11, 14 June 1791, as cited in Isabel Bourdin, *Les Société populaires à Paris pendant la Révolution*, (Paris: Librairie du Recueil Sirey, 1937), 140. For the Cercle Sociale, see Gary Kates, *The Cercle Social, the Girondins, and the French Revolution* (Princeton, N.J.: Princeton University Press, 1985).

8 Ibid.

9 Ibid.

10 *Réglement de la Société Fraternelle des Minimes*, in *Les Femmes dans la Révolution française*, vol. 2.

11 See Duhet, *Les Femmes*, 103.

12 *Réglement.*
13 *Extrait des Déliberations de Société fraternelle des deux sexes*, 4 December, 1791, in de Villiers, *Clubs des femmes*, 51.

14 Ibid., 42.

15 Ibid.

16   Duhet, *Les Femmes*, 115-116.

17   *Discours prononcé à la Société Fraternelle des Minimes*, in Soboul's *Les Femmes dans la Révolution française*, vol. 2.

18   Ibid.

19   *La Gazette universelle*, 7 and 17 July, as cited as Rosa, *Citoyennes*, 83.

20   Ibid.

21   Bourdin, *Sociétés populaires*, 145.

22   Rosa, *Citoyennes*, 82.

23   Bourdin, *Société populaires*, 146-147.

24   *Patriote français*, 1 April 1791, as cited in Bourdin, *Société populaires*, 147.

25   Rosa, *Citoyennes*, 82.

26   *Bouche de Fer*, no. 64.

27   *Bouche de Fer*, no. 1.

28   *Révolutions de Paris*, no. 143, mars 31 à avril 7, 1792.

29   According to de Villiers, *Clubs des Femmes*, 38, Etta Palm d'Aelders lived quietly in Holland and later was arrested there (1795) when the Batavian Republic was declared and spent almost three years in prison.

30   For a discussion of this declaration, see further this chapter.

31   *Archives parlementaires*, 34:289.

32   Ibid., 41:63-64.

33   Elizabeth Racz, "The Women's Rights Movements in the French Revolution," *Science and Society* 16 (1951-52): 151-174.

34   The most comprehensive treatment is that of Evelyne Sullerot, *Histoire de la presse*

féminine en France, des origines à 1848 (Paris: Armand Colin, 1966), 42-86.

35   As cited ibid., 48.

36   Ibid., 46-54.

37   Ibid., 54-55.

38   See Jeremy Popkin, *Revolutionary News: The Press in France, 1789-1799* (Durham, N.C.: Duke University Press, 1990).

39   For more details on Madame Roland, see her *Memoires.*

40   Rudé, *Crowd*, 99-100.

41   Claude Manceron in preface to Olivier Blanc, *Olympe de Gouges* (Paris: Editions Syros, 1981), 5.

42   *Le Prince Philosophe* quoted in Benoîte Groult, ed., *Œuvres de Olympe de Gouges* (Paris: Mercure de France, 1986), 215.

43   *Départ de M. Necker et Madame de Gouges,* in Groult, *Œuvres,* 97.

44   *Déclaration*, in Groult, *Œuvres,* 102.

45   Quoted in Blanc, *Olympe,* 133-134.

46   *La Fierté de l'innocence,* as quoted in Lairtullier, *Femmes célèbres,* 108.

47   Ibid., 106-107.

48   *Révolutions de Paris,* 15 July, 1792.

49   *Les Fantômes de l'opinion publique,* as cited in Blanc, *Olympe,* 144.

50   *Pronostic sur Maximilien Robespierre, par un animal amphibie* as quoted in Blanc, *Olympe,* 144.

51   *Compte moral,* as cited in Blanc, *Olympe,* 147.

52   *Moniteur,* 14:751-752.
53   *Révolutions de Paris,* no. 180, 22 December, 1792.

54 Lacour, *Trois Femmes,* 59.

55 *L'Entrée de Dumouriez à Bruxelles ou les vivandiers* as quoted in Blanc, *Olympe,* 154.

56 *Complots dévoilés* as quoted in Blanc, *Olympe,* 155.

57 *Avis pressant* as quoted in Blanc, *Olympe, 156.*

58 *Testament politique* as quoted in Lairtullier, *Femmes célèbres,* 129.

59 *Testament politique* as quoted in Lacour, *Trois femmes,* 64.

60 Lairtullier, *Femmes célèbres,* 128.

61 *Défense d'Olympe de Gouges face au Tribunal Révolutionnaire,* in Groult, *Œuvres,* 125.

62 Ibid.

63 Lairtullier, *Femmes célèbres,* 130.

64 Report of police spy La Tour-la-Montagne in Tuetey, *Répertoire géneral,* 9:416-417, document no. 1367.

65 As cited by Soprani, *La Révolution et les femmes,* 166.

66 Lairtullier, *Femmes célèbres,* 133.

67 *Moniteur,* 18:326. She habitually deducted seven years from her age.

68 Ibid., 18: 343-344.

69 Ibid., 18: 450.

70 Blanc, *Olympe,* 125.

71 Otto Ernst, *Théroigne de Méricourt, d'après des documents inédits tirés des archives secrètes de la maison d'Autriche* (Paris: Payot, 1939); Marcellin Pellet, *Etude historique et biographique sur Théroigne de Méricourt* (Paris: Maison Quantin, 1886); Ferdinand de Strobl-Ravelsberg, ed., *Les Confessions de Théroigne de Méricourt, la fameuse*

amazone révolutionnaire (Paris: Louis Westhauser Editions, 1898); Elizabeth Roudinescu, *Théroigne de Méricourt: une femme mélancolique sous la Révolution* (Paris: Seuil, 1989).

72 Lairtullier, *Femmes célèbres*, 55.

73 de Strobl-Ravelsberg, *Confessions*, 76.

74 Ibid., 95.

75 Ibid.

76 Ibid., 118.

77 Lairtullier, *Femmes célèbres*, 63.

78 de Strobl-Ravelsberg, *Confessions*, 118-119.

79 See Lacour, *Trois femmes*, 106-107, for examples.

80 de Strobl-Ravelsberg, *Confessions*, 120.

81 Procédure criminelle, witness no. 91.

82 de Strobl-Ravelsberg, *Confessions*, 119.

83 Ibid., 158.

84 Ibid., 123.

85 Ibid., 161.

86 Aulard, *Jacobins*, 3:346.

87 *Le Patriote français*, 4 February, 1792.

88 *Journal des débats et de la correspondance de la Société des amis de la constitution*, 4 February, 1792 as quoted in Lacour, *Trois femmes*, 54.

89 *Discours prononcé à Société Fraternelle des Minimes le 25 mars, 1792, l'an quatrième de la liberté* in *Les Femmes dans la Révolution française*.

90 Ibid.

91   Lacour, *Trois femmes*, 281, cites Lamartine as one author who described this scene.

92   *Souvenirs de la terreur* as cited by Lacour, *Trois femmes*, 281.

93   See Roudinescu, *Théroigne de Méricourt*, 125.

94   Ibid., 124.

95   Pellet, *Etude historique et biographique*, 98.

96   Ibid.

97   *Moniteur*, 13: 538.

98   *Aux 48 sections*, B.N. folio B.N. Lb41-4940.

99   Tuetey, *Répertoire général*, 9:174, document no. 598. Also see document nos. 13 and 351.

100   Roudinesco, *Théroigne de Méricourt*, 152.

101   Godineau, *Tricoteuses*, 116.

102   Beaulieu, *Essais historiques sur les causes et les effets de la Révolution* (Paris; 1801-19) as cited in Pellet, *Etude historique*, 98.

103   Joseph Vaesen, *Révolution française: Lyon en 1791. Notes et documents*, vol. 4 (Lyon: Henri Georg, n.d.): 55.

104   Ibid.

105   Maurice Wahl, *Les Premières années de la révolution à Lyon, 1788-92* (Paris: Armand Colin, 1892), 365.

106   Ibid.

107   *Révolutions de Paris*, no. 185, 19-26 January, 1793, 295.

108   Wahl, *Premières années*, 366.

109   Ibid.

110   *Journal de Lyon*, 9 January, 1793, 25-26.

111   Ibid., 26.

112   Ibid., January 10, 1793, 30.

113   *Révolutions de Paris*, no. 185, 19-26 January, 1793, 235.

114   Ibid.

115   *Journal de la société populaire*, no. 21, 335-336.

116   Wahl, *Premières années*, 606

117   Bill Edmons, "The Rise and Fall of Popular Democracy in Lyon, 1789-1795," *Bulletin of the John Rylands University Library of Manchester* 67 (1984): 408-449. Equally devoid of information on the women of Lyon are the detailed studies by Richard Cobb, *Les Armées révolutionnaires: Instrument de la Terreur dans les départements, avril 1793 - floréal An II*, 2 vols. (Paris: Mouton, 1961-63), and C. Riffaterre, *Le Mouvement antijacobin et antiparisien à Lyon et dans le Rhône-et-Loire en 1793 (29 mai 15 août)*, 2 vols. (Paris, 1912, 1928).

118   Robert R. Palmer, *Twelve Who Ruled: The Year of the Terror in the French Revolution* (Princeton, N.J.: Princeton University Press, 1941), 168, 169, 174.

NOTES TO CHAPTER 3

1   Aulard, *Jacobins*, 5:37.

2   Ibid.

3   Michelet, *Femmes*, 72.

4   *L'ami de peuple*, 30 December, 1890.

5   Tuetey, *Répertoire général*, 9:vi.

6   *Moniteur*, 15:544.

7   *Moniteur*, 16:362.

8   *Discours prononcé à la barre de l'Assemblée Nationale par Madame Claire Lacombe*, 25 July 1793, in A. Soboul, ed., *Les Femmes dans la Révolution française*. For a brief treatment of Léon and Lacombe, see R.B. Rose, *The Enragées: Socialists of the French Revolutuion?* (Melbourne: Melbourne University Press, 1965), chapters 5 and 6.

9   *Moniteur*, 13:248.

10   *Archives parlementaires*, 48:714 and Tuetey, *Répertoire général, report no. 2281, 9:283.*

11   Cerati, *Club des Citoyennes*, 36.

12   Aulard, *Jacobins*, 5:123.

13   Cerati, *Club des Citoyennes*, 39.

14   Ibid., 41-43.

15   Ibid., 40.

16   Lacour, *Trois femmes*, 356.

17   Quoted in Lacour, *Trois femmes*, 355, and taken from the library of Paul Lacombe.

18   Godineau, *Tricoteuses*, 131.

19   Aulard, *Jacobins*, 5:186.

20   Cerati, *Club des Citoyennes*, 54, from *Journal des Debats*, 14 May 1793.

21   Ibid.

22   De Villiers, in *Clubs des Femmes,* says that "this women's club, organized solely for cooperation in the overthrow of the Girondins, merits no toleration," 228.

23   Aulard, *Jacobins*, 5:198.

24   Ibid., 5:199. The *Courrier des Départements* reported on the 22 that this speech was delivered by a woman. This is cited by de Villiers, *Clubs des Femmes*, 233.

25   Aulard, *Jacobins*, 5:198.

26   Cerati, *Club des Citoyennes*, 54.

27   Aulard, *Jacobins*, 5:212.

28   Godineau, *Tricoteuses*, 34.

29   Tuetey, *Répertoire général*, 8:415, doc. no. 2642.

30   Ibid., 9:597.

31   For a fuller discussion of this situation, see Olivier Blanc, *Olympe de Gouges.*

32   *Moniteur*, 16:421.

33   Ibid.

34   Ibid.

35   Ibid.

36   Ibid. Marat replied with these words: "This is the plan of the Roland woman."

37   Ibid.

38   Ibid., 16:432.

39 Tuetey, *Répertoire général,* 9:186, doc. no. 617.

40 Cited in Cerati, *Club des Citoyennes*, 56-57.

41 Godineau, *Tricoteuses*, 137.

42 Tuetey, *Répertoire général*, doc. no. 645, 9:196.

43 Cerati, *Club des Citoyennes*, 58.

44 Ibid., 59.

45 Godineau, *Tricoteuses*, 137.

46 Ibid, 136.

47 Cerati, *Club des Citoyennes*, taken from the memoires of Meillan.

48 *Moniteur*, 16:527.

49 Even so close a student of the Revolution as Morris Slavin overlooks this report in the *Moniteur* and implies that this incident was revealed more than a year afterwards. See his *The Making of an Insurrection: Parisian Sections and the Gironde* (Cambridge: Harvard University Press, 1986), 147.

50 Godineau, *Tricoteuses*, 138.

51 *Moniteur*, 16:543.

52 Cerati, *Club des Citoyennes,* 60.

53 Godineau, *Tricoteuses*, 138.

54 Ibid. This idea of women armed to the teeth was insisted upon by many of the Girondins in the weeks that followed.

55 Cerati, *Club des Citoyennes*, 60, 61.

56 Quoted by Slavin, *Making of an Insurrection*, 136. It might be noted that not even Rudé has been able to provide an analysis of the insurgents of May 31-June 1793. See *Crowd*, 122-25.

57   *Discours prononcé à la société des républicaines révolutionnaires par les citoyennes de la section des droits de l'homme,* in *Les Femmes dans la Révolution française.*

58   *Moniteur,* 16:731.

59   Cerati, *Club des Citoyennes,* 92.

60   Ibid., 94, from Dossier Lacombe AN TI. 001-1-3.

61   Ibid., 95-96.

62   Ibid., 27.

63   De Villiers, *Clubs des Femmes,* 226-27.

64   Report of the police spy Dutard in Tuetey, *Répertoire général,* 9:204, document no. 659.

65   Gorsas in *Courrier des départements,* 20 mai 1793.

66   *Moniteur,* 17:661.

67   Ibid., 17:679.

68   Ibid., 16:669.

69   *Réglement* issued July 9. Reproduced in Lacour, *Trois Femmes,* 355 but from the private papers of Paul Lacombe.

70   Ibid.

71   Godineau, *Tricoteuses,* 131.

72   Ibid.

73   Prousinalle (P.J.A. Roussel), *Le Château des Tuileries ou récit de ce qui s'est passé dans l'intérieur de ce palais, depuis sa construction jusqu'à 18 Brumaire de l'an VIII.* Paris: Chez Lerouge, 1802.

74   Ibid., 38.

75   Ibid., 39.

76 Ibid.

77 Ibid., 41.

78 Ibid., 42-43.

79 *Moniteur*, 16:762.

80 Ibid., 16:762.

81 Ibid., 16:758.

82 Ibid., 16:754.

83 Ibid., 17:2. The names of women arrested on June 28 and imprisoned in la Force due to rioting and for pillaging soap were published here.

84 Godineau, *Tricoteuses*, 141.

85 *Moniteur*, 17:151.

86 Cerati, *Citoyennes*, 105.

87 Tuetey, *Répertoire général*, 9:252, document 765.

88 *Moniteur*, 17:230.

89 *Moniteur*, 17:299. Minutes of the *conseil general,* July 31.

90 Cerati, *Club des Citoyennes*, 102.

91 *Moniteur*, 17:120.

92 J.L. David, *Rapport et décret pour la fête du 10 août*, as cited in Godineau, *Tricoteuses*, 148.

93 Tuetey, *Répertoire général,* 9:263, document no. 821.

94 *L'Ami du peuple*, August 8, 1793.

95 Aulard, *Jacobins*, 5:356.

96   Ibid., 5:360.

97   *Archives parlementaires*, 19:83.

98   Godineau, *Tricoteuses*, 152.

99   *Moniteur*, 17:503-04.

100   Godineau, *Tricoteuses*, 159.

101   Tuetey, *Répertoire général*, 9:364-365, document no. 1222.

102   Tuetey, *Répertoire général,* 9:368, document no. 12223

103   Durham, "Sans-jupons' Crusade," 278.

104   *Moniteur*, 17:580.

105   Ibid., 17:580-81.

106   See Palmer, *Twelve Who Ruled*, 44-45, for a good discussion.

107   Petition to the Jacobin Club on September 13.

108   Aulard, *Jacobins*, 5:484.

109   Report of police observateur Le Harivel in Tuetey, *Répertoire général*, 9:395, document no. 1306.

110   *Moniteur,* 17:661.

111   Godineau, *Tricoteuses*, 120.

112   Report of police spy Beraud in Tuetey, *Répertoire général*, 9:422, document number 1357.

113   Report of police spy Rousseville in Tuetey, *Répertoire général*, 9:422, document no. 1388.

114   Tuetey, *Répertoire général*, 9:413, document number 1357.

115   Ibid., document no. 1359.

116   *Moniteur*, 17:717.

117   Ibid., 17:718.

118   Report of la Tour-la-Montagne in Tuetey, *Répertoire général*, 9:420-21, document no. 1381.

119   Report of Le Harivel in Tuetey, *Répertoire général*, 9:421, document no. 1383.

120   Report of Rousseville in Tuetey, *Répertoire général*, 9:422, document no. 1388.

121   Aulard, *Jacobins*, 5:486.

122   Ibid.

123   Ibid., 5:407.

124   *Moniteur*, 17:695.

125   Ibid., 696.

126   *Rapport fait par la Citoyenne Lacombe à la Société des Républicaines Révolutionnaires de ce qui s'est passé le 16 septembre à la société des Jacobins*, in Soboul, ed., *Les Femmes dans la Révolution française*.

127   *Moniteur*, 18:62.

128   Ibid., 69.

129   Aulard, *Jacobins*, 5:451.

130   Tuetey, *Répertoire général*, 10:117-18.

131   *Moniteur*, 18:290.

132   Ibid.

133   Ibid., 299, 300.

134   Ibid.

135   *Archives parlementaires*, 78:364.

136 *Moniteur*, 18:450

NOTES TO CHAPTER 4

1   Donald Greer, *The Incidence of the Terror During the French Revolution: A Statistical Interpretation* (Gloucester, Mass., 1966; Harvard University Press: 1935), 96.

2   Albert Soboul and Raymonde Monnier, *Répertoire du personnel sectionnaire parisien en l'an II* (Paris: Publications de la Sorbonne, 1985).

3   Ibid., 386.

4   Ibid., 189, 149, 169.

5   Godineau, *Tricoteuses*, 293.

6   See ibid., 294 for details of some meetings.

7   *Moniteur*, 24: 326-27 and Kare Tønnesson, *La Défaite des sans-culottes: mouvement populaire et réaction bourgeoise en l'an III* (Paris: Librairie R. Clavreuil, 1959), 154 and Chapter 5.

8   *Gazette Français*, 21 pluviose, in A. Aulard, *Paris pendant la réaction Thermidorienne et sous le directoire* (Paris: Cerf, 1898), 467.

9   Godineau, *Tricoteuses*, 294.

10   Aulard, *La Réaction thermidorienne*, 1:363.

11   *Moniteur*, 23:297.

12   Aulard, *La Réaction thermidorienne,* 1:348.

13   C. Marand-Fouquet, *La Femme au temps de la Révolution* (Paris: Stock/Laurence Pernoud, 1989), 277.   Also see *Moniteur*, 23:717.

14   Godineau, Tricoteuses, 299.

15   *Le Reveil Républicain par une democrate* in Soboul,ed., *Les Femmes dans la Révolution,* vol. 2.

16   Godineau, *Tricoteuses*, 298.

17   Aulard, *La Réaction thermidorienne*, 1:596.

18   Ibid., 1:597.

19   Ibid., 1:609.

20   Ibid., 1:589.

21   *Moniteur*, 24:36.

22   Aulard, *La Réaction thermidorienne,* 1:604.

23   *Moniteur*, 24:79.

24   Ibid.

25   Ibid., 24:85.

26   Ibid.

27   Ibid., 85-86.

28   Ibid., 87.

29   Aulard, *La Réaction thermidorienne,* 1:615.

30   Godineau, *Tricoteuses*, 302.

31   *Moniteur*, 24:113.

32   Ibid., 114.

33   Ibid.

34   Ibid.

35   Ibid., 115.

36   Ibid.

37   Ibid., 119.

38   For details see Tønnesson, *Défaite*, chapter 9.

39   Aulard, *La Réaction thermidorienne*, 1:720-21.

40   Ibid., 1:723.

41   Godineau, *Tricoteuses*, 306.

42   Aulard, *La Réaction thermidorienne*, 1:724.

43   Ibid., 1:733-34, 727.

44   Godineau, *Tricoteuses*, 307.

45   Ibid., 309.

46   Aulard, *La Réaction thermidorienne*, 1:728.

47   Ibid., 1:729. The assignants at this time had depreciated to 8% of their demarcated value.

48   Ibid., 1:730.

49   Ibid.

50   Reproduced in E. Tarlé, *Germinal and Prairial* (Moscow: Editions en langues étrangères, 1959), 368-69.

51   Godineau, *Tricoteuses*, 320.

52   Ibid.

53   *Le Courrier Républicain*, in Aulard, *La Réaction thermidorienne*, 1:736.

54   Godineau, *Tricoteuses*, 321.

55   *Messager du soir*, 2 prairial, in Aulard, *La Réaction thermidorienne*, 1:735.

56   Ibid.

57   *Courrier républicain*, in Aulard, *La Réaction thermidorienne*, 1:735.

58   *Messager du soir*, in Aulard, *La Réaction thermidorienne*, 1:735.

59   Ibid.

60   *Moniteur*, 24:501.

61   Ibid., 501-02.

62   Ibid., 502.

63   Ibid.

64   Ibid.

65   Ibid.

66   Rudé, *Crowd*, 153.

67   *Moniteur*, 24:502-03.

68   Ibid., 504.

69   Tønnesson, *Défaite*, 270.

70   Aulard, *La Réaction thermidorienne*, 1:733.

71   See Tønneson, *Défaite*, 270.

72   Rudé, *Crowd*, 154.

73   Godineau, *Tricoteuses,* 328.

74   *Détails circonstanciés*, Général Kilmaine, as cited in Tønneson, *Défaite,* 315n.

75   Ibid.

76   Godineau, *Tricoteuses*, 328-29.

77   Aulard, *La Réaction thermidorienne*, 1:741.

78   Godineau, *Tricoteuses*, 325.

79   Aulard, *La Réaction thermidorienne*, 1:743.

80   See Godineau, *Tricoteuses*, Chapter 2 of Part 4, 305-332, "Les Boutefeux" for an excellent discussion of the women's participation.

81   Aulard, *La Réaction thermidorienne*, 1:746.

82   Report of police spy Castille as cited in Godineau, *Tricoteuses*, 329.

83   Ibid., 330.

84   Ibid.

85   Aulard, *La Réaction thermidorienne*, 1:733.

86   Tarlé, *Germinal*, 369.

87   Aulard, *La Réaction thermidorienne*, 1:733.

88   See Monnier and Soboul, *Répertoire* for an abundance of evidence to support the arguments.

89   Ibid., 529, 428.

90   Ibid., 533.

91   Ibid., 335.

92   *Moniteur*, 24:515.

93   Ibid.

94   Ibid., 519.

95   Ibid., 542.

NOTES TO CONCLUSION

1   Godineau in her article in *Rebel Daughters* delineates three categories of women.

2   Quoted in Bouvier, *Les Femmes pendant la Révolution,* 110.

BIBLIOGRAPHY

I. PRIMARY SOURCES

A. Archival Material

Archives Nationale:

AEII 1250—Dossier of Pauline Léon.

AF46—Report on Théroigne de Méricourt.

C267 638—Petition des Citoyennes républicaines révolutionnaires, 16 August 1793.

F7 3686(6)—Women's riot in Lyon, September, 1792.

F7 4693—Femme Duney, Germinal Year III.

F7 4756—Dossier of Claire Lacombe.

F7 4774 14—Femme Legros, Germinal Year III.

F7 4774—Femme Parisel, Germinal Year III.

B. Official printed sources

Archives parlementaire de 1787 à 1860, recueil complet des débats législatifs et politiques des Chambres françaises, imprimé par order du Sénat et de la Chambre des députés, Première série (1787 à 1700). 82 vols. Paris: Librairie administrative de P. Dupont, 1862-; Washington, D.C.: Microcard Editions, 1967.

Réimpression de l'ancien Moniteur, 32 vols. Paris: H. Plon, 1858-63.

C. Contemporary Newspapers

L'Ami du Peuple

Le Babillard

La Bouche de Fer

Le Courrier de l'Hymen

Les Entrennes Nationales des Dames

La Feuille du Soir

La Gazette des Halles

Journal de Lyon

La Mère Duchesne

Le Patriote français

Révolutions de France et de Brabant

Les Révolutions de Paris

D. Collections of primary sources

Aulard, F.A., ed., *Paris pendant la réaction thermidorienne et sous le Directoire*. 5 vols. Paris: 1898-1902.

___, *La Société des Jacobins: Recrueil de documents pour l'histoire du Club des Jacobins de Paris*. 6 vols. Paris: 1889-97.

Buchez, B.J. et P.C. Roux, eds., *Histoire parlementaire de la Révolution française, ou journal des Assemblées nationales, depuis 1789 jusqu'en 1815*. 40 vols. Paris: 1834-38.

Caron, Pierre. *Paris pendant la Terreur: Rapports de agents secrets du Ministre de l'intérieur*. 4 vols. Paris: 1910-1949.

Duhet, Paule Marie, ed., *Cahiers de doléances des femmes en 1789 et autres textes*. Paris: Des Femmes, 1981.

La Croix, Sigismund, ed., *Actes de la commune de Paris pendant la Révolution*. Vol. 2. Paris: L. Cerf, 1895.

Tuetey, Alexandre, ed., *Répertoire général des sources manuscrites de l'histoire de Paris pendant la Révolution française.* 11 vols. Paris: Imprimerie nouvelle, 1890-1914.

Walter, Gérard, ed., *Actes du tribunal révolutionnaire.* Paris: Mercure de France, 1968.

E. Edhis reprinted sources

Soboul, Albert, ed., Les Femmes dans la Révolution française 1789-94. 70 imprimés reproduits in-extenso, pétitions, pamphlets, affiches, documents divers. 2 vols. Paris: Edhis, 1982.

"Adresse individuelle à l'assemblée nationale par des citoyennes de Paris, 27 fevrier, 1792."

"Le Cri du sage par une femme (Olympe de Gouges)."

"Discours prononcé à la barre de l'assemblée nationale par Madame Claire Lacombe, 25 juillet, 1792."

"Discours des citoyennes françoises, prononcé à la société des amis de la constitution séante aux Jacobins, à Jacobins, à Paris, 18 décembre, 1791."

"Discours préliminaire de la pauvre Javotte."

"Discours prononcé à la Société Fraternelle des Minimes, le 25 mars 1792, l'an quatrième de la liberté par Mlle. Théroigne en presentant un drapeau aux citoyennes du Faubourg S. Antoine."

"Entrennes Nationales des dames par M. de Pussy et une Société de Gens-de-Lettres. No. 1 du 30 novembre, 1789."

"Evénement de Paris et de Versailles par une des Dames qui à eu l'honneur d'être de la Députation à l'assemblée générale."

"Les Héroines de Paris, 5 octobre, 1789."

"Lettres d'une Citoyenne à son amie sur les avantages que procurerait à la nation: le patriotisme des dames, Paris, Chez la veuve Lambert, 1789."

"Motions adresses à l'assemblée nationale en faveur du sexe."

"Motion à faire et arrêt à prendre dans les differentes classes et corporations de citoyennes françaises. Septrembre, 1789."

"Pétition des Citoyennes républicaines révolutionnaires lue à la barre de la convention nationale.

"Le Partisan de l'égalité politique entre les individus ou problem très-important de l'égalité en droits et de l'inégalité en fait par Pierre Guyomard."

"Pétition des femmes à l'assemblée nationale."

"Rapport fait par la Citoyenne Lacombe à la société des républicaines révolutionnaires."

"Requête des dames à l'assemblée nationale."

"Réglement de la société fraternelle."

"Du Sort actuel des femmes."

F. Other primary sources

Bailly, Jean Sylvain, *Mémoires d'un témoin de la Révolution.* 3 vols. Paris: Baudouin Frères, 1821.

Campan, Madame. *Mémoires sur la vie privée de Marie-Antoinette, reine de France et de Navarre suivis de souvenirs et anecdotes historiques sur les règnes de Louis XIV, de Louis XV et de Louis XVI.* Paris: Baudouins Frères, 1823.

de Gouges, Olympe. *Œuvres de Madame de Gouges dédiées à monseigneur le Duc d'Orléans*, 2 vols. Paris: Chez l'auteur, Chez Cailleau, 1788. (Microfilm).

de Gouges, Olympe. *Œuvres*. Benoîte Groult, ed., Paris: Mercure de France, 1886.

de Strobl-Ravelsberg, Ferdinand, ed., *Les Confessions de Théroigne de Méricourt, la fameuse Amazone révolutionnaire. Extrait du procès-verbal inedit qui fut dressé à Koufstein (Tyrol) en 1871*. Paris: Louis Westhauser, 1892.

Hardy, S., *Mes Loisirs, ou journal d'événements tels qu'ils parviennent à ma connoissance*. Vol. 8. Paris: 1789.

Marquise de la Tour du Pin, *Mémoires de la Marquise de la Tour du Pin: Journal d'une femme de cinquante ans (1778-1815) suivis d'extraits inédits de sa correspondance (1815-1846)*. Paris: Mercure de France, 1989.

Memoires secrètes de Fournier l'Américain, ed. F.A. Aulard. Paris: Société de l'histoire de la Révolution française, 1890.

Mounier, J.J., *Appel au Tribunal de l'opinion publique, du rapport de M. Chabroud, et du décret rendu par l'Assemblée Nationale le 2 Octobre 1790, sur les crimes du 5 et du 6 octobre 1789*. Genéva: 1790.

Procédure criminelle, instruite au Châtelet de Paris, sur la dénonciation des faits arrivés à Versailles dans la journée du 6 octobre, 1789. Paris: Chez Baudouin, 1790

Prousinalle (P.J.A. Roussel). *Le Château des Tuileries ou récit de ce qui s'est passé dans l'intérieur de ce palais, depuis sa construction jusqu'à 18 Brumaire de l'an VIII*. Paris: Chez Lerouge, 1802.

Récit de ce qui s'est passé à Versailles et à Paris depuis le lundi 5 jusqu'au vendredi 9 octobre 1789, envoyé par un témoin authentique et oculaire. Reproduced in *Revue historique* 84 (1904): 296-306.

Vaesen, Joseph, ed. *Révolution française: Lyon en 1791. Notes et documents. Vol. IV. Publiés par Albert Metzger et révisés par Joseph Vaesen*. Lyon: Librairie generale Henri Georg.

II. SECONDARY WORKS:

A. Books and Dissertations:

Abensour, Leon, *La Femme et le féminisme avant la Révolution.* Paris: Leroux, 1923.

Agulhon, Maurice, *Marianne au combat: L'imagerie et la symbolique républicaines de à 1880.* Paris: Flammarion, 1979.

Albistur, Maité and Daniel Armogathe, *Histoire du Féminisme Français du Moyen Age à Nos Jours.* Paris: Editions des femmes, 1977.

Bell, Susan G., and Karen M. Offen, eds., *Women, the Family, and Freedom: the Debate in Documents.* Vol. 1. Stanford, California: Stanford University Press, 1983.

Berkin, Carol R. and Clara M. Lovett, *Women, War, and Revolution.* New York: Holmes & Meier, 1980.

Bertaud, Jean-Paul, *Les Amis du roi: journaux et journalistes royalistes en France de 1789 à 1792.* Paris: Perrin, 1984.

Bessand-Massenet, Pierre, *Femmes sous la révolution: la fin d'une société.* Paris: Plon, 1953.

Bourdin, Isabelle. *Les Sociétés populaires à Paris pendant la révolution.* Université de Paris, Centre d'études de la révolution française série des études historiques. Paris: Librairie du Recueil Sirey, 1937.

Bouvier, Jeanne. *Les Femmes pendant la révolution: leur action politique, sociale, économique, militaire, leur courage devant l'échafaud.* Paris: Editions Eugène Figuière, 1931.

Braesch, F., *La Commune du dix août 1792.* Paris: 1911; Genève: Mégariotis Reprints, 1978.

Branca, Patricia, *Women in Europe since 1750.* New York: St. Martin's Press, 1978.

Brinton, Crane, *A Decade of Revolution, 1789-1799*. New York: Harper & Brothers, 1961.

Blanc, Olivier, *Olympe de Gouges*. Paris: Editions Syros, 1981.

Bruhat, Y., *Les Femmes de la révolution française*. Paris: 1939.

Cerati, Marie, *Le Club des Citoyennes Républicaines Révolutionnaires*. Paris: Editions Sociales, 1966.

Cobb, Richard, *Les Armées révolutionnaires: Instrument de la Terreur dans les départements, avril 1793 - floréal An II*. 2 vols. (Paris: Mouton, 1961-63).

___, *A Second Identity: Essays on France and French History*. New York: Oxford University Press, 1969.

Connelly, Owen, *The French Revolution and Napoleonic Era*. 2nd ed. Fort Worth, Texas: Holt, Rinehart and Winston, Inc., 1991.

de Villiers, Marc. *Histoire des clubs de femmes et des légions d'amazones*. Paris: Plon, 1910.

___, *Les 5 et 6 Octobre 1789: Reine Audu (les légendes des journées d'octobre)*. Paris: Emile-Paul Frères, 1917.

Doyle, William, *The Oxford History of the French Revolution*. Oxford: Clarendon Press, 1989.

Dubroca, Louis, *Les Femmes célèbres de la révolution*. Paris: 1802.

Duhet, Paule Marie, *Les Femmes et la révolution 1789-1798*. Paris: Juillard, 1971.

Durham, Mary Jay. "The Sans-Jupons' Crusade for Liberation duing the French Revolution." Ph.D. dissertation, Washington University, 1972.

Egret, Jean, *Révolution des Notables: Mounier et les Monarchiens, 1789*. Paris: Librairie Armand Colin, 1950.

Ernst, Otto, *Théroigne de Méricourt, d'après des documents inédits tirés des Archives secrètes de la maison d'Autriche*. Paris: Payot, 1935.

Farge, Arlette, *La Vie fragile: Violence, pouvoirs et solidarités à Paris au XVIIIe siècle*. Paris: Hachette, 1986.

Fleishman, Hector, *Les Femmes et la terreur d'après les archives nationales*. Paris: 1910.

Furet, François and Denis Richet, *The French Revolution*. London: 1970.

Furet, François and Mona Ozouf, *Dictionnaire critique de la Révolution française*. Paris: Flammarion, 1988.

Fusil, Louise, *Souvenirs d'une actrice*. Paris, 1846.

Garrioch, David, *Neighbourhood and Community in Paris, 1740-1790*. Cambridge University Press, 1986.

Gendron, François, *La Jeunesse dorée: Episodes de la révolution française*. Sillery: Presses de l'Université du Quebec, 1979.

Godineau, Dominique, *Citoyennes tricoteuses: Les femmes du peuple à Paris pendant la Révolution française*. Aix-en-Provence: Alinea, 1988.

Goland, Fernand, *Les Féministes françaises*. Paris, 1925.

Goncourt, E. and J., *La Femme au XVIII siècle*. 2 vols. Paris, 1882.

Goodwin, A., *The French Revolution*. London: Hutchinson University Library, 1966.

Gottschalk, Louis and Margaret Maddox, *Lafayette in the French Revolution: Through the October Days*. Chicago: the University of Chicago Press, 1969.

Hamel, Frank. *A Woman of the Revolution: Théroigne de Méricourt*. London: Stanley Paul and Co., n.d.

Harris, Robert D., *Necker and the Revolution of 1789.* Lanham, New York, London: University Press of America, 1986.

Hedman, Edwin R., "Early French Feminism from the Eighteenth Century to 1848." Ph.D. dissertation, New York University, 1954.

Higgins, F.L., ed., *The French Revolution as Told by Contemporaries.* Cambridge: The Riverside Press (Houghton Mifflin), 1938.

Hufton, Olwen, *Women and the Limits of Citizenship in the French Revolution.* Toronto: University of Toronto Press, 1992.

Hunt, Lynn, *Politics, Culture, and Class in the French Revolution.* Berkeley: University of California Press, 1984.

Kates, Gary, *The Cercle Social, the Girondins, and the French Revolution.* Princeton, New Jersey: Princeton University Press, 1985.

Kelly, George Armstrong, *Victims, Authority, and Terror: The Parallel Deaths of d'Orléans, Custine, Bailly, and Malesherbes.* Chapel Hill, North Carolina: University of North Carolina Press, 1982.

Kelly, Linda, *Women of the French Revolution.* London: Hamish Hamilton, 1987.

Kennedy, Michael, *The Jacobin Clubs in the French Revolution. The First Years.* Princeton, New Jersey: Princeton University Press, 1982; *the Middle Years.* Princeton, New Jersey: Princeton University Press, 1988.

Lacour, Leopold, *Les Origines du Féminisme Contemporaine: Trois Femmes de la Révolution, Olympe de Gouges, Théroigne de Méricourt, Rose Lacombe.* Paris: Librairie Plon, 1900.

Levy, Darline Gay, Harriet Applewhite and Mary Durham Johnson, *Women in Revolutionary Paris, 1789-1795.* Urbana, Illinois: University of Illinois Press, 1979.

Lairtullier, E., *Les femmes célèbres de 1789 à 1795, et leur influ- ence dans la révolution, pour servir de suite et de complément à toutes les histoires de la révolution française.* 2 vols. Paris: Chez France, à la librairie politique, 1840.

Landes, Joan B., *Women and the Public Sphere in the Age of the French Revolution.* Ithaca, New York: Cornell University Press, 1988.

Lasserre, Adrien, *La Participation collective des femmes à la révolution française: les antécédents du féminisme.* Paris: Felix Alcan, 1906.

LeClercq, Henri, *Les journées d'octobre et la fin de l'année 1789.* Paris: Librairie Letouzey et Ane, 1924.

Lefebvre, Georges, *The Coming of the French Revolution.* Princeton, New Jersey: Princeton University Press, 1947, 1967.

___, *The Thermidorians.* New York: Random House, 1966.

___, *The French Revolution.* 2 vols. New York: Columbia University Press, 1962.

Marand-Fouquet, Catherine, *La femme du temps de Révolution.* Paris: Stock/Laurence Pernoud, 1989.

Mathiez, Albert, *Le Club des Cordeliers pendant la crise de Varennes et le massacre du Champ de Mars.* Paris: Champion, 1910.

May, Gita, *Madame Roland and the Age of Revolution.* New York: Columbia University Press, 1970.

Melzer, Sara and Leslie Rabine, eds., *Rebel Daughters: Women and the French Revolution.* New York: Oxford University Press, 1992.

Michelet, Jules, *Les Femmes de la Révolution.* 7th ed. Paris: Calmann Levy, 1889.

Monnier, Raymonde, *Le Faubourg Saint-Antoine (1789-1815)*. Paris: Société des Etudes Robespierristes, 1981.

Moses, Claire Goldberg, *French Feminism in the Nineteenth Century*. Albany, New York: SUNY Press, 1984.

Outram, Dorinda, *The Body and the French Revolution: Sex, Class and Political Culture*. New Haven and London: Yale University Press, 1989.

Ozouf, Mona, *La Fête révolutionnaire, 1789-1799*. Paris: Gallimard, 1976.

Palmer, R.R., *Twelve Who Ruled: The Year of the Terror in the French Revolution*. Princeton, New Jersey: Princeton University Press, 1941.

Pellet, Marcellin, *Etude historique et biographique sur Théroigne de Méricourt*. Paris: Maison Quantin, 1886.

Popkin, Jeremy, *Revolutionary News: The Press in France, 1789-1799*. Durham, North Carolina: Duke University Press, 1990.

Rendall, Jane, *The Origins of Modern Feminism: Women in Britain, France and the United States, 1780-1860*. Chicago: Lyceum Books, 1985.

Rice, Howard C., *Thomas Jefferson's Paris*. Princeton, New Jersey: Princeton University Press, 1976.

Riffaterre, C., *Le Mouvement antijacobin et antiparisien à Lyon et dans le Rhône-et-Loire en 1793 (29 mai 15 août)*, 2 vols. Paris, 1912, 1928; Geneva: Mégariotis Reprints, 1979.

Robertson, George M., "The Society of the Cordeliers and the French Revolution." Ph.D. dissertation, University of Wisconsin, 1972.

Rose, R.B., *The Enragés: Socialists of the French Revolution?* Melbourne: Melbourne University Press, 1965.

Roudinesco, Elisabeth, *Théroigne de Méricourt: Une femme mélancolique sous la Révolution*. Paris: Seuil, 1989.

Rudé, George, *The Crowd in the French Revolution*. London: Oxford University Press, 1959.

Schama, Simon, *Citizens: A Chronicle of the French Revolution*. Toronto: Random House, 1990.

Schmidt, Adolphe, *Paris pendant la révolution d'après les rapports de la police secrète, 1789-1800*. Vols. I and II. Translated by Paul Viollet. Paris: Champion librairie, 1880.

Slavin, Morris. *The French Revolution in Miniature: Section Droits-de-l-Homme, 1789-1795*. Princeton, New Jersey: Princeton University Press, 1984.

___, *The Making of an Insurrection: Parisian Sections and the Gironde*. Cambridge, Massachusetts: Harvard University Press, 1986.

Soboul, Albert, *The French Revolution, 1787-1789, from the Storming of the Bastille to Napoleon*. New York: Vintage Books, 1975.

___, *Les San-culottes parisiens en l'an II: Mouvement populaire et gouvernement révolutionnaire, 2 juin 1793-9 thermidor an II*. Paris: Librairie Clavreuil, 1958.

Sokolnika, Galian O., *Nine Women Drawn from the Epoch of the French Revolution*. Translated by H.C. Stevens. Essay Index Reprint Series. Freeport, New York: Books or Libraries Press, 1969 [1932].

Soprani, Anne, *La Révolution et les femmes*. Paris: M.A. Editions, 1988.

Sullerot, Evelyne, *Histoire de la presse féminine en France des origines à 1848*. Paris: Librairie Armand Colin, 1966.

Spencer, Samia, ed., *French Women in the Age of Enlightenment*. Bloomington, Indiana University Press, 1984.

Sutherland, D.M.G., *France 1789-1815: Revolution and Counterrevolution*. London: Fontana Paperbacks and William Collins, 1985.

Sydenham, M.J., *The First French Republic, 1792-1804*. London: B.T. Batsford, 1974.

___, *the French Revolution*. London: B.T. Batsford, 1965.

___, *The Girondins*. London: Athlone Press, 1961.

Tarlé, E., *Germinal et Prairial*. Moscow: Editions en Langues Etrangères, 1959.

Tønnesson, Kare D., *La Défaite des Sans-Culottes: Mouvement populaire et réaction bourgeoise en l'an III*. Paris: Librairie R. Clavreuil, 1959.

Tulard, Jean and Jean-François Fayard and Alfred Fierro, *Histoire et dictionnaire de la Révolution Française, 1789-1799*. Paris: Robert Laffont, 1987.

Vray, Nicole, *Les Femmes dans la tourmente*. Paris: Editions Ouest-France, 1988.

Wahl, Maurice, *Les premières années de la révolution à Lyon, 1788-1792*. Paris: Armand Colin, 1894.

B. Articles:

Abray, Jane, "Feminism in the French Revolution," *American Historical Review* 80 (1975): 43-62.

Colwill, Elizabeth, "Just Another Citoyenne? Marie-Antoinette on Trial, 1790-1793." *History Workshop: A Journal of Socialist and Feminist Historians* 28 (Autumn, 1989): 63-87.

Desan, Suzanne, "The Role of Women in Religious Riots during the French Revolution." *Eighteenth Century Studies* 22 (Spring, 1989), 451-68.

Devance, L., "Féminisme pendant la Révolution Française." *Annales historiques de la Révolution française*. 49 (1977): 342-76.

Edmonds, Bill, "The Rise and Fall of Popular Democracy in Lyon, 1789-1795," *Bulletin of the John Rylands University Library of Manchester* 67 (1984): 408-49.

George, Margaret, "The World Historical Defeat of the Republicaines Révolutionnaires." *Science and Society* 40 (Winter 1976-77): 410-37

Godineau, Dominique, "Masculine and Feminine Political Practice during the French Revolution, 1793-Year III," in Harriet Applewhite and Darline Levy, eds., *Women and Politics in the Age of the Democratic Revolution*. Ann Arbor: University of Michigan Press, 1990, 61-80.

Graham, Ruth, "Loaves and Liberty: Women in the French Revolution," in Renate Bridenthal and Claudia Koontz, eds., *Becoming Visible: Women in European History*. Boston: Houghton Mifflin, 1977, 236-54.

Hufton, Olwen, "Women in the French Revolution, 1789-1796," *Past and Present* 53 (1971): 90-108.

___, "Women in Revolution, 1789-1796," in Douglas Johnson, ed., *French Society and the Revolution*, Cambridge University Press, 1976, 148-66.

___, "Women in Revolution," *French Politics and Society*, 7, No. 3 (Summer, 1989): 65-81.

___, "Voilà la citoyenne," *History Today* 39 (May, 1989): 26-33.

Johnson, Mary Durham, "Old Wine in New Bottles: The Institutional Changes for Women of the People during the French Revolution," in Carol R. Berkin and Clara M. Lovett, eds.,*Women, War, and Revolution*. New York: Holmes & Meier, 1980, 107-43.

Kadane, Kathryn A., "The Real Difference between Manon Phlipon and Madame Roland," *French Historical Studies* 3 (1964): 542-49.

Levy, Darline G. and Harriet B. Applewhite, "Women and Political Revolution in Paris," in Renate Bridenthal, Claudia Koonz and Susan Stuard, eds., *Becoming Visible: Women in European History*, 2nd ed., Boston: Houghton Mifflin, 1987, 281-306.

___, "Women, Democracy, and Revolution in Paris 1789-94," in Samia Spencer, ed., *French Women and the Age of Enlightenment*.. Bloomington: Indiana University Press, 1984, 64-79.

___, "Women of the Popular Classes in Revolutionary Paris, 1789-1795," in Carol R. Berkin and Clara M. Lovett, eds.,*Women, War, and Revolution*. New York: Holmes & Meier, 1980, 9-36.

___, "Women, Radicalization, and the Fall of the French Monarchy," in Harriet Applewhite and Darline Levy, eds., *Women and the Age of the Democratic Revolution*. Ann Arbor: University of Michigan Press, 1990, 81-107.

Lyttle, Scott H., "The Second Sex (September 1793)," *Journal of Modern History* 27 (1955): 14-26.

Mathiez, A., "Etude critique sur les journées des 5 et 6 octobre 1789." *Revue historique* 67 (1898): 241-81; 68 (1899): 258-94; 69 (1899): 41-66.

Monnier, Raymonde, "Les Sociétés populaires dans le département de Paris sous la révolution." *Annales historiques de la Révolution française* 278 (1989): 356-73.

Racz, Elizabeth, "The Women's Rights Movement in the French Revolution," *Science and Society* 16 (1951-52): 151-74.

Scott, Joan Wallach, "French Feminists and the Rights of the Man: Olympe de Gouges' Declarations." *History Workshop: A Journal of Socialist and Feminist Historians* 28 (Autumn, 1989): 1-21.

Sewell, William H., "Le citoyen/la citoyenne: Activity, Passivity, and the Revolutionary Concept of Citizenship," in Colin Lucas, ed., *The French Revolution and the Creation of Modern Political Culture, Vol. 2, The Political Culture of the French Revolution.* Oxford: Pergamon, 1988.

Soboul, Albert, "Sur l'Activité militante des femmes dans les sections Parisiennes en l'an II," *Bulletin d'histoire economique et sociale de la Revolution Française* 2 (1979): 15-25.

Thomas, Chantal, "Heroism in the Feminine: The Examples of Charlotte Corday and Madame Roland," in Sandy Petrey, ed., *The French Revolution 1789-1989: Two Hundred Years of Rethinking.* Lubbock, Texas: Texas Tech University Press, 1989.

INDEX

O

P

T

Studies in Modern European History

The monographs in this series focus upon aspects of the political, social, economic, cultural, and religious history of Europe from the Renaissance to the present. Emphasis is placed on the states of Western Europe, especially Great Britain, France, Italy, and Germany. While some of the volumes treat internal developments, others deal with movements such as liberalism, socialism, and industrialization which transcend a particular country.

The series editor is:

Frank J. Coppa
Director, Doctor of Arts Program
in Modern World History
Department of History
St. John's University
Jamaica, New York 11439